Utopian Visionaries

PROFILES

Utopian Visionaries

Thomas Streissguth

The Oliver Press, Inc.
Minneapolis

0 3 6 5 7 3 9 2

The Oliver Press, Inc.
Charlotte Square
5707 West 36th Street
Minneapolis, MN 55416-2510

Library of Congress Cataloging-in-Publication Data

Streissguth, Thomas, 1958-
Utopian visionaries / Thomas Streissguth.
p.   cm.—(Profiles)
Includes bibliographical references and index.
    Summary: Discusses efforts to create perfect societies by such
individuals as: Ann Lee and Joseph Meacham and the Shakers,
Christian Metz and the Amana Colonies, George Rapp and the
Harmony Society, Robert Owen and New Harmony, George
Ripley and Brook Farm, John Humphrey Noyes and Oneida, and
Katherine Tingley and the Point Loma community.
ISBN 1-881508-47-1 (lib. bdg.)
    1. Utopias—History—Juvenile literature. [1. Utopias.]
I. Title II. Series: Profiles (Minneapolis, Minn.) ; 29.
HX806.S77 1999
321'.07—DC21
[B]   98-2533
                                                    CIP
                                                    AC

ISBN: 1-881508-47-1
Printed in the United States of America

05 04 03 02 01 00 99   8 7 6 5 4 3 2 1

Contents

Sir Thomas More (1478-1535) envisioned a society governed by reason for the good of all citizens. A victim of the passions of his time, More was executed for standing up for his Roman Catholic beliefs.

6

Introduction

*T*hinking about the modern world can be distressing. Nations fight wars. Societies are torn apart by economic, political, and religious conflict. Millions of people suffer from violence and poverty. While some live comfortably, many more endure hunger and disease.

Many of us are too preoccupied with our own problems to care about these crises. We shrug our shoulders and say, "What can we do?" Others talk about change, but they do not put their ideas into action. A few, however, do something—they build their own utopias.

For thousands of years, philosophers and writers have been creating imaginary worlds that are superior to the ones they live in. The ancient Greek philosopher Plato planned one such ideal society in his book *The Republic*. The English writer Sir Thomas More coined the term *utopia*, a Greek word meaning "no place," in *Utopia*, a short book he wrote in 1516. More's Utopia was an island nation in the newly discovered West Indies. People in his imaginary society enjoyed much better living conditions than those in Europe at that time.

Although More's Utopia was fictitious, the New World was fact, and European explorers and settlers were beginning to sail there in large numbers. In many ways, the Americas represented a utopian opportunity—vast and unexplored land where people could start over and build the perfect society. They could try new civic institutions and social arrangements in this wilderness. Utopian visionaries with new doctrines could lead their followers without interference or persecution. Instead of an imaginary place, Utopia could become a reality.

Over the next few centuries, many small religious groups crossed the Atlantic Ocean from Europe. Pilgrims from England, Huguenots from France, and Anabaptists from central Europe built new communities in the forests and plains of North America. All were seeking safety from the persecution and violence brought about by the clashes of competing religious beliefs. Among the fleeing Protestant sects were the Shakers, who would become one of the largest and most successful utopian societies in the New World.

After she became the Shaker sect's leader, an English mystic named Ann Lee brought her followers to America. Lee arrived in 1774, just before the American Revolution.

Fined or jailed for leaving the Church of England, the Pilgrims came to America to build a society in which they could worship in peace.

Another revolution was then brewing in America, and the Shakers would be leaders in it. The Second Great Awakening, a religious movement led by preachers who were breaking away from long-established Protestant churches, began in the 1790s. Instead of sitting on hard church pews in stuffy buildings, their congregations met under revival tents in the countryside. Instead of giving solemn lectures, preachers inspired their listeners with spontaneous, fiery sermons. Crowds wept and prayed aloud, and the Shakers would become so moved during services that they would begin to dance and shake. No longer were the mysteries of religion solely in the hands of church officials and ordained ministers—the followers of the Second Great Awakening experienced firsthand visions and miracles like those seen by biblical prophets.

Not long after the beginning of the Second Great Awakening, a German pastor named George Rapp established self-sufficient Harmony Society communities in Pennsylvania and Indiana. Living by strict rules and entrusting Rapp with absolute authority, Harmonists flourished in the early nineteenth century.

As the Harmonists busied themselves in their small industries, population growth and industrialization brought new problems to American society. Many urban workers lived in poverty, barely supporting their families. A much smaller class of factory owners, meanwhile, enjoyed vast wealth. Such economic inequalities prompted some social reformers to invent more *egalitarian* utopias, in which everyone would share equally and have a decent standard of living.

In the 1820s, Scottish businessman and social reformer Robert Owen sought to create an egalitarian society in the United States. His successful experiment in New Lanark, Scotland, gave him both the money he needed and the motivation to develop a new community. Owen bought Harmony in Indiana from George Rapp and remade the religious utopia into New Harmony.

Following in the footsteps of his countryman George Rapp, German religious leader Christian Metz brought his Inspirationists to the United States in the early 1840s. The Inspirationists, who belonged to a sect

Many religious utopians in the nineteenth century were convinced that the Second Coming of Christ would soon occur. They imagined greeting their savior as the people of Jerusalem did so long ago, by scattering palm leaves and shouting "Hosanna!"

known as the Pietists, eventually sought solitude in Iowa, where they built a community of seven small towns.

While the Inspirationists molded their lives to their biblical teachings, a Boston minister named George Ripley formed a small utopia based on cooperative work and intellectual stimulation. Ripley was strongly influenced by the philosophy of Transcendentalism, which held that human beings could achieve new insights by following their own instincts. He combined study, manual labor, and group recreation at a small Massachusetts community named Brook Farm, which attracted many contemporary writers, including Nathaniel Hawthorne.

While many utopians rejected facets of modern society, one group caused a furor by redefining the institution of marriage. A religious utopian named John Humphrey Noyes imagined a community in which each member strived for perfection in God's eyes through selflessness. Men and women would share all that they had—including their spouses. But since the Oneida community was formed in a time when adultery was against the law, members risked prosecution. Nevertheless, Noyes was able to avoid legal problems for many years. His community's manufacturing industry was also a financial success.

There were hundreds of other utopian communities in the United States, but nearly all had disappeared by the beginning of the twentieth century. The rise in property values and growth of big business made it more difficult for utopian visionaries to obtain land, market their goods, and attract new members. Katherine Tingley, however, managed to found the Theosophical community of Point Loma near San Diego, California. Theosophy held that people could improve themselves by studying the divine wisdom at the heart of the world's major religions. Point Loma's Theosophists were to be a model for other Theosophical communities around the world.

In the 1960s, a new wave of utopian communities sprouted in the United States as people sought to escape the nation's fast-paced, competitive economy. Thousands of young people turned against the government and big business and "dropped out" of history's wealthiest society. These utopians sought to live a simpler life that offered spiritual instead of material rewards. Some believed in *anarchism*—opposition to any established government, law, or authority. Others tried to create *communistic* societies, in which all resources were held in common. Some utopians of the 1960s also founded the food and housing cooperatives that still exist in many cities and towns.

Today, utopians can plan their societies using computer games such as Sim City, My City, or Civilization. Players of these games must shape a society from scratch or grapple with a troubled city, facing the challenges of structuring an economy, limiting pollution, and ensuring public safety. Several such games have online versions on the Internet, allowing players to interact with each other.

The Internet also offers utopians a chance to meet and discuss their ideas with like-minded people all over the world. Their plans may include ingenious solutions to social problems like epidemic disease, environmental devastation, and poverty. But utopian societies in the virtual reality of a computer game or the Internet do not face the same obstacles as the nineteenth-century utopias. Instead of building their societies by punching a keyboard, utopians of the past had to carve their communities out of the wilderness, often facing a harsh climate, hostile neighbors, and economic hardship. Their lives are examples of vision and determination.

Shakers pose at New York's Mount Lebanon community in the 1880s, over a century after Ann Lee led the religious group to America. There are no known images of Ann Lee or of Joseph Meacham.

1

Ann Lee and Joseph Meacham
The Shakers

*O*dd noises were disturbing the people of the English town of Manchester. Rumors of witchcraft and bizarre ceremonies spread through the countryside. More than once neighbors called in the local constables to put a stop to the strange rites and throw the leaders of the group in jail. Other times mobs attacked the worshippers.

James and Jane Wardley, the leaders of these services, were members of a Protestant sect that had broken away from the Quakers. Known as the Shaking Quakers, or Shakers, their beliefs had been influenced by the

Camisards, also known in French as *les Trembleurs*—"the Tremblers." The Camisards had been a sect of dissident Protestants residing in the Cévennes region of southern France in the early 1700s. Like the Shakers, they had experienced signs and manifestations of the Holy Spirit. After years of persecution at the hands of France's Roman Catholic authorities, they fled to England in 1706. Although the Camisards had disappeared over the next few decades, their example of religious devotion and fearless defiance of oppressors was inspiring.

During the Wardleys' religious services, men and women would shake, shout, and run wildly about the room in a frenzy. Members of their small congregation fell into deep trances and spoke in incomprehensible "tongues." They heard voices and told prophecies of the Second Coming of Christ, which they believed would occur at any moment.

In the 1770s, a woman named Ann Lees became the leader of the Wardleys' small group of Shakers in Manchester. Few official records of her early life exist. According to tradition, she was born on February 29, 1736, and she worked as a fur-cutter in Manchester when she was a young woman. In September 1758, she joined the Wardleys' congregation, attracted by their direct and emotional communication with God. Four years later, she married a blacksmith named Abraham Standerin. Early in her marriage, she endured four difficult births. Each time, her child died in infancy.

Believing these deaths to be divine punishment for a sinful life, Lees experienced an overwhelming sense of guilt and dismay. Terrifying hallucinations tormented her, and she tried to atone for her sins by giving up food, sleep, shelter, and all other earthly comforts. She came to view marriage and sex as the worst of sins—immoral acts that had brought about disease, famine, war, slavery, and all human misery.

In 1773, Ann Lees and several other Shakers were arrested when they interrupted an Anglican church service. Unable to pay the heavy fine for disturbing the peace, Lees went to prison. There she experienced powerful visions and heard mysterious voices. The voices said that God was both male and female. Christ, she was told, was one of the highest spirits and had appeared as a male in Jesus; now Christ had arrived as a female and mother in Lees herself. To the Wardleys and the other Shakers, Lees's suffering and her vision made her the congregation's true spiritual leader. The members confessed all their past sins to her and began following her rule of strict *celibacy*, or life without sexual relations.

Nine months after Ann Lees was released from jail, a Shaker believer named James Whittaker also had a vision. He saw a large tree with brightly shining leaves, which to him represented the American colonies. Ann Lees and the Shakers believed the vision was a sign from God. They soon prepared to sail for the distant English colonies in North America. In May 1774, Ann Lees and

While the Virgin Mary is revered by Christians as the mother of Jesus Christ, the Shaker followers of Ann Lees honored "Mother Ann" as the maternal or feminine part of Christ.

eight members of the sect left for America. Among the group were Whittaker; Lees's brother William and niece Nancy; and Ann Lees's husband, Abraham Standerin (who had not yet joined the Shakers). After surviving two months of stormy and dangerous weather crossing the Atlantic Ocean, the group landed in New York City.

While Ann Lees stayed behind in the city, her followers traveled north along the Hudson River valley in search of a site for a new home. They finally settled on a place named Niskeyuna, northwest of the city of Albany. There they cleared a small acreage and built a log cabin. In the spring of 1776, Ann Lee (she had now dropped the "s" from her last name) finally arrived at Niskeyuna.

The Shakers came to America in the years before the Second Great Awakening, a series of religious revivals that would sweep the small towns of New England and New York for decades. The fervor was already beginning in the late 1770s, and the Shakers would be leaders in this rebirth of faith. One revival in New Lebanon, a town near Niskeyuna, attracted hundreds in the summer of 1779. Signs of the Second Coming had appeared to some Baptists in the congregation of Joseph Meacham there. But in early 1780 the revivalists grew disillusioned when the promised Judgment Day failed to arrive. Searching for divine guidance, Meacham sent a friend named Calvin Harlow to visit Ann Lee and the Shakers, who, sharing Meacham's faith, had named themselves the "United Society of Believers in Christ's Second Appearing."

At Niskeyuna, Harlow asked how a woman—who the Bible says must obey her husband—could lead a Christian congregation. But Lee's husband had abandoned her after arriving in New York. "When the man is gone," Mother Ann answered, "the right of government belongs to the woman." Later, while visiting the Shaker congregation, Meacham saw unmistakable signs that Mother Ann Lee and the Shakers were preaching the true faith. He heard prophecies in otherworldly voices and saw faith-healing of fevers, broken bones, and incurable diseases. That summer, word of the miracles spread, and a stream of visitors came to Niskeyuna to witness the Shaker meetings. The visitors observed ceremonies that began with a simple hymn and soon proceeded to dancing, shaking, running, and jumping in place. Worshippers shouted and spoke in strange tongues. Impressed by the Shakers' devotion, Meacham and several of his followers in New Lebanon converted to Shakerism.

Shakers danced, according to one eyewitness, "in imitation of the angels around the throne of God."

But others in the area grew suspicious. The Revolutionary War was raging, and these strange English Shakers could be using their meetings to hide acts of espionage and treason. Ann Lee and her followers refused to aid the American cause or serve in the Continental army fighting the British. Worse, their doctrines of celibacy and full confession reminded many local farmers and townspeople—most of whom were Protestant—of the hated Roman Catholic Church. The Shakers' strange rites resembled those of witches, and their faith-healing seemed nothing more than black magic.

In July 1780, local police jailed Ann Lee and several of her disciples, hoping to end the turmoil the Shaker meetings were causing. But their action backfired. After spending several weeks in jail without being charged, the Shakers began to win sympathy throughout New York and New England. Weren't the colonists fighting England for the same freedoms that were being denied to the Shakers? New York governor George Clinton issued the Shakers a reprieve.

The next spring, Lee took advantage of her popularity to lead a missionary journey through New England. She and other Shaker leaders preached in Connecticut, Massachusetts, New Hampshire, and Maine. Although many opposed them—sometimes with violence—others were converted. The services inspired dozens of farmers and artisans to leave their traditional churches, confess their sins to Ann Lee, and join the United Society.

One of these converts, James Jewett of Enfield, New Hampshire, donated his farm to the Shakers. There the Shakers built a settlement, pooling all of their money and property and organizing themselves into several "families." These families were loosely structured communities with between a few dozen and several hundred members who shared food and labored cooperatively.

As more family units were formed, Ann Lee and James Whittaker created guidelines for independent Shaker communities. They required members to give up all of their private property and family ties and move to a Shaker settlement. Regular confession and simple living would gradually rid members of worldly striving and desires. Then, the Shakers believed, they could reach spiritual perfection while still on earth—a state they believed Mother Ann already had attained.

Over the next three years, the United Society continued to grow. Wherever a new colony was established, local farmers and townspeople visited the Shakers, curious to learn about their doctrines and wondering whether Lee's followers had found the true faith. But the troubles of the Shakers' early years and the difficulties she experienced in New York took their toll on Mother Ann. The death of her brother William in July 1784 proved to be an especially hard blow for her. Two months later, on September 8, 1784, Ann Lee died. Upon Mother Ann's death, James Whittaker took her place as head of the Shaker community.

Whittaker spent the next two years organizing new Shaker families and establishing new communities on land donated by converts. He appointed the town leaders and wrote the many rules for daily living and personal conduct that the sect would follow over the next century. Under his leadership, the Shakers built their first meeting house in 1785 at Mount Lebanon, Joseph Meacham's community in New Lebanon.

The Mount Lebanon community. Shaker men and women lived at the dwelling house on the left, near the curved-roofed meeting house in which they worshipped. The trustees' office (the dark building on the right) housed the store and rooms for visitors.

In 1787, James Whittaker died. The Shakers were still a small sect, uncertain of how best to organize themselves for the future. They elected Meacham to be their new leader. "Joseph is my first Bishop," Ann Lee had once declared. "He will have the keys of the Kingdom; he is my apostle in the ministry." Her prophecy convinced the Shakers that Meacham had been chosen by God and by Mother Ann to guide them. Meacham's leadership and organizational skills made Shakerism an institution that could continue after the death of Ann Lee.

Under Joseph Meacham's direction, the Shakers separated themselves completely from the outside world in September 1787. Establishing a self-sufficient religious utopia, Meacham believed, was the best way to avoid the hostility and corrupting influences of non-Shakers. A few months later, all of the Shakers gathered at Mount Lebanon to celebrate a Christmas dinner that marked the founding of Meacham's Shaker utopia.

A total of 11 separate Shaker settlements were established in New York, Connecticut, Massachusetts, New Hampshire, and the territory of Maine. Each included several families of about 60 members each, equally divided between men and women. Each family was supervised by a male and a female elder and had its own buildings and land. The families would be self-supporting, producing all the food and goods they needed. The largest Shaker community, located at Mount Lebanon, was home to as many as eight families at one time.

Shaker girls weaving straw mats. To Shakers, labor was a form of worship and a way to avoid sin.

Meacham also divided the Shakers into two separate and equal branches, male and female. Lucy Wright was named the head of the female line of Shakers. Men and women had separate workshops; they ate apart in the dining halls; and they slept in different sections of the dwelling houses. The two sexes were further isolated during the 1790s, and contact between them was strictly controlled. All meeting places had separate entrances for men and women, and during social evenings they would take seats along the opposite sides of a room for general conversation and the singing of hymns. The sexes also stayed in separate groups at Shaker services, when energetic dancing and shouting took place.

On the basis of their spiritual development, members were divided into orders. Those who lived the purest lives and had the strongest faith belonged to the senior order. The junior order included less spiritually advanced or younger members. New members and children reached the junior order after a period of instruction. Those whose tasks brought them into contact with the outside world were in the outer order.

The Shakers attracted a steady stream of new members over the next few decades. Some arrived at the Shaker settlements out of curiosity; others sought to escape the fast-paced life in the growing eastern cities. New members had to confess their sins to the elders and spend a period of probation with a Shaker family. Before becoming full-fledged members of a Shaker community, they had to settle all debts and turn over their property to the family. Prospective members who were married had to have the consent of their wives or husbands to end their marriages.

In addition to the elders who managed the Shaker families, there were male and female trustees and deacons who handled Shaker property and business affairs. Other managers directed the workshops, mills, stores, and farms. The Shakers believed that members should learn a variety of tasks. Their many small workshops and factories were kept neat and clean, with tools hung on

Shaker chairs are so esteemed for their fine craftsmanship that they are now considered works of art and are prized by collectors and museums.

pegs on the walls when not in use. Members produced furniture, shoes, brooms, and leather goods, and they spun cloth to make clothing. The goods were always of simple design and solid construction. The Shakers believed that simplicity was an outward sign of holiness, so all unnecessary ornament and decoration—from picture frames to fancy woodcarving—was prohibited.

Shaker products earned a good reputation and found a ready market in New England's towns and villages. Talented inventors, the Shakers created or improved many labor-saving devices, including the circular saw and the threshing machine for harvesting grain. The Shakers also invented the flat broom—a broom with its bristles arranged in a long, flat row—the clothespin, and the screw propeller later used in boat and airplane motors.

Within the Shaker communities, goods were distributed to the members of each family through a general store. Trustees managing the property and economy of the towns gathered products from the Shaker farms and workshops and bought any necessary supplies, such as steel plows or horses. They distributed the goods to the

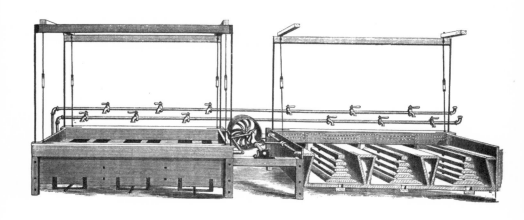

The Shaker community of Canterbury, New Hampshire, displayed this washing machine at the 1876 Centennial Exhibition in Philadelphia.

deacons, who passed them out to individual members as needed. Members of the Shaker families were only entitled to what they needed for a simple life, as determined by the deacons, and detailed records were kept that showed what each individual received.

Joseph Meacham died in 1796. Under his leadership, the Shakers had grown from the small and scattered Shaker communities formed by Mother Ann and James Whittaker into the prosperous and growing United Society. Because of Meacham's efforts, the Shakers would flourish for many years.

In the early nineteenth century, with 11 communities already thriving in the Northeast, the Shakers sent a group of missionaries to the Ohio and Kentucky region, which at that time was the country's western frontier. The Shakers hoped to take advantage of a religious revival that was sweeping the lands along the Ohio River valley.

They faced strong opposition at first, especially from ministers who accused them of breaking up marriages and families. But gradually the missionaries won converts. Groups of Shaker converts were "gathered" into new families and settled on land either bought or donated by one of the members. The first Ohio River valley community was built at Union Village, near Lebanon, Ohio, in 1806. Shaker farms in Ohio flourished, and new communities were soon established there and across the Ohio River in Kentucky. The Mount Lebanon community founded a Shaker settlement as far away as Florida.

In the 1850s, Shaker communities peaked at about 4,000 members, and Shaker towns were often the wealthiest and most orderly places on the rough-and-tumble western frontier. As the years passed, however, the Shakers came under increasing pressure to conform to a rapidly industrializing society. Under the leadership of Elder Frederick Evans at Mount Lebanon, who guided the society through the years during and after the Civil War, the community's contact with the outside world increased. The Shakers began distributing their goods by railroad and steamship rather than by horse-drawn cart.

Gradually, some of the strict rules of the early Shakers were relaxed, but Mount Lebanon continued to enforce the basic rules laid down by Ann Lee and Joseph Meacham: celibacy, confession, and isolation from the surrounding society.

The principle of celibacy meant that children were not born Shakers, so the Shakers constantly had to recruit new members from the outside world. But many children brought into the community by converts had no interest in living a simple, frugal, devout life in the countryside, and they left when they became adults. Often there was also conflict between leaders and ordinary members, who began to rebel against the expectation of strict obedience. At the same time, the Shakers' communal life was losing much of its attractiveness for the population at large.

After the Civil War, the communities began to decline. The Ohio River valley settlements disappeared

Frederick Evans had been a radical journalist, an atheist, and a member of Robert Owens's New Harmony utopia. He became a Shaker in 1831 because Shakers practiced equal treatment of women, blacks, and ethnic minorities.

altogether as the Shakers sold off their land and buildings. By the early twentieth century, the number of Shakers had fallen to just a few hundred aging members in the oldest communities of the Northeast. Unable to sustain itself, the Mount Lebanon community disbanded after World War II. Two small communities of Shakers continued at Canterbury, New Hampshire, and Sabbathday Lake, Maine. In the 1990s, seven members remained in the community of Sabbathday Lake.

Searching for the ideal place to await the Second Coming of Christ, George Rapp (1757-1847) led his followers from Germany to the United States, where they eventually settled three different communities.

32

2

George Rapp
The Harmony Society

*O*n Independence Day 1804, the *Aurora* sailed into
Baltimore's harbor after its long voyage from Europe.
Like many other ships of the time, the *Aurora* was carrying hundreds of immigrants to the United States. Here,
they believed, they could work and worship without fear
of persecution.

One group of passengers stood apart from the rest.
Three hundred Germans, most of them farmers and
craftspeople, were heading for a tract of wilderness in the
forested hills of western Pennsylvania. These immigrants

came not to make their fortunes, but to surrender all their money and possessions. Instead of claiming land and building homes of their own, they would share everything. They did this willingly and happily under the guidance of their spiritual leader, George Rapp.

Rapp was born on October 28, 1757, in the town of Iptingen, located in the kingdom of Württemburg in what is now southwestern Germany. Like most of his followers, Rapp was a *vine dresser*, a person who cultivated grape vines. He learned this skill as a young man, working in his family's vineyards. From his early years, Rapp was very religious and lived strictly according to biblical teachings.

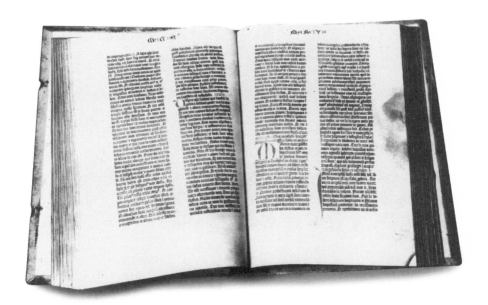

Rapp wanted to model his life after the early Christians he read about in the Bible.

Although Martin Luther (1483-1546) originally hoped to reform the Roman Catholic Church, he ended up creating a new church that allowed parishioners to interpret the word of God for themselves.

When he grew up, he and his own family faithfully attended the town's Lutheran church.

A former monk, Martin Luther had founded the Lutheran Church nearly three centuries earlier because he wanted to bring people closer to God. Many clergy members in the Catholic Church lived in luxury, and they delivered their sermons in Latin, an ancient language incomprehensible to most people. Lutherans, in contrast, held services in the native language of parishioners.

By George Rapp's time, the Lutheran Church was a powerful institution. Rapp felt the church had become unresponsive to its members. The church's leaders, Rapp believed, were lazy and corrupt, and he found the rituals of the service repetitious and empty. Rapp yearned for sermons addressing problems that concerned the congregation. Turning away from his church at about the age of 30, Rapp began preaching his own sermons to a small circle of friends in his home.

Rapp believed that true Christians should follow the example of the early apostles of the New Testament. The first Christians had given up all their possessions and even left their families to follow Jesus and his teachings. In order to create a Christian community, Rapp felt that he and his followers should also give up all their money and property to the group. Each member would then labor for the good of the community. Such a community would flourish apart from society, raising its own food and earning money from the production of its own workshops. Isolated from the everyday world of competition, selfishness, and greed, members would find true happiness and harmony by living according to Christian doctrine. Their Christian community would then be ready for the Second Coming, when Jesus Christ would reappear on earth and pass a final judgment on all people. Rapp believed this event would happen soon.

As more people came to Rapp's house to listen to his sermons, the Lutheran churches of Württemburg grew empty. The alarmed ministers of the region demanded action by the civil authorities (there was no separation of church and state in Württemburg in the late 1700s). For not attending the Lutheran church services on Sunday, members of Rapp's flock found themselves hauled into local courts, facing fines and time in jail. Nevertheless, they remained devoted to Rapp. They would follow his instruction, no matter where it led them. Rapp refused to return to the Lutheran Church, and his growing circle of followers would not stop attending his sermons.

The persecution continued for years. Gradually, Rapp came to the conclusion that he and his followers would have to leave Württemburg. In 1803, Rapp was finally ready to act. Selling all of his property, he sailed to the United States with his son John, leaving his followers behind to wait until he sent for them. In America Rapp hoped to find a place where he and his followers could live according to the Bible.

In October 1803, Rapp arrived in Philadelphia on the ship *Canton*. For several months, he searched rural Pennsylvania for good, cheap land on which to build his Christian utopia. Finally, Rapp found a tract of wilderness about 12 miles from the Ohio River in Butler County and arranged to buy 3,000 acres. He wrote a letter to his close friend Frederick Reichert, sending for his followers.

Frederick Reichert had stayed in Iptingen to look after the affairs of the several hundred followers. A traveling stone mason, Reichert had become a member of Rapp's congregation after hearing him preach in Iptingen. Reichert was also a skilled business manager to whom Rapp could entrust the financial problems and details of the community. Rapp remained the sole spiritual leader. Under Reichert's guidance, the people sold their property and homes in Württemburg and prepared for the long ocean crossing.

In July and September of the following year, some 650 of Rapp's followers arrived in Philadelphia and Baltimore. While most of them moved into temporary homes in Philadelphia, about 80 men and women set out with Rapp and Reichert for Butler County. They cleared the land of trees and raised log cabins for the new settlers. Finally, in February 1805, the rest of the community came and assembled by Connoquenessing Creek in the young town that became known as Harmony (then spelled "Harmonie").

At a founding meeting on February 15, Rapp and Reichert drew up a document called the Articles of Association, which formally established the Harmony Society. According to the Articles of Association, members agreed to turn all their money and property over to George Rapp and his associates. In return, Rapp would provide food, shelter, schooling, and religious guidance. Members who decided to leave the society would be reimbursed for their contribution.

George Rapp was so close to Frederick Reichert that he adopted him as his son. From that time on, Frederick took the name Frederick Rapp. George Rapp became known as Father Rapp because he was considered the father of the whole society.

The first two years at Harmony were not easy since food was in short supply. But Father Rapp's strong spiritual influence held the group together. Because of Frederick Rapp's persistence in establishing agriculture and industry, the Harmonists survived the lean times. It was not long before the members of the society were raising new homes, a church, and a barn. As they cleared more land, they built a distillery for making alcohol, a sawmill for planing lumber, and a tannery for processing leather. They planted a vineyard, and they also bought a flock of sheep to raise for wool. Harmonist farms were soon yielding large crops of grains, fruits, and vegetables.

At Harmonist church services, members sang hymns and studied the Bible.

Frederick Rapp arranged to sell Harmony's surplus food in nearby towns and bought more land.

In 1807, the younger members of the Harmony Society decided they wanted to adopt a life of celibacy. As with all important decisions, they first consulted Father Rapp. Harmony's founder pondered the idea carefully and concluded that the celibate person would be better prepared for the Second Coming. But he advised them to proceed cautiously with such a major change.

Eventually, all members of Harmony followed the youths' lead. Men and women who were already married still lived in the same house, but they saw themselves no longer as married couples but as brothers and sisters in God's family. Even without new children being born at Harmony, the community continued to grow as outsiders joined the Harmonists.

By 1810, the Harmonists had cleared over 2,000 acres of land and raised 130 buildings in their town. Under the guidance of Frederick Rapp, the Harmonists prospered from selling their livestock, whiskey, and grain to the region's farmers and townspeople. But both he and Father Rapp had grown unhappy with Harmony's location. The soil was too infertile and the weather too cold for growing grapes. Because there were few neighbors still willing to sell their land cheaply, there was also little space available for expansion. Furthermore, it was a difficult 12-mile ride to the Ohio River, the main route for transporting the society's goods.

Father Rapp was also worried about the spiritual state of his followers. Now that the hard work of clearing the land and constructing the buildings was finished, the Harmonists were growing too comfortable. Idleness threatened, as well as discontent with the society's strict doctrines and rules. In 1814, Father Rapp set out down the Ohio River to find a new tract of wilderness to tame on what was then the western frontier.

Looking for uncleared land with access to the Ohio River, Father Rapp searched in southwestern Indiana near the town of Vincennes. He finally found a good site on the Wabash River, which fed into the Ohio. He could get

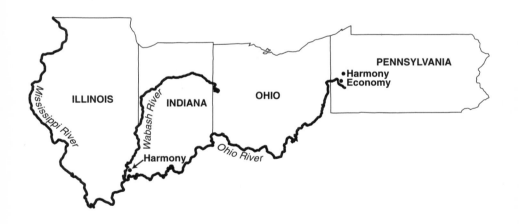

To attain better access to rivers for transporting goods, the Harmonists moved from Harmony, Pennsylvania, to the banks of the Wabash River and founded Harmony, Indiana. From there, they could deliver their products on the Ohio and Mississippi Rivers.

25,000 acres of land there for less than $3 an acre. He stayed at the new site with two other men, while another group came from Harmony to clear the land and begin building new homes.

According to Frederick Rapp's plan, the new Indiana town, also known as Harmony (or "Harmonie"), was laid out in a square. The first homes and shops were built by the group along the outer edges of the square. Gradually, they expanded inward toward the center, where Father

Since the Harmonists were now celibate, their homes at Harmony, Indiana, resembled dormitories.

In addition to their success in agriculture, the Harmonists excelled in a number of areas of industry. Here, community men take a break from their work at a planing mill.

Rapp's house stood at the main intersection. Warehouses were built to hold the household goods that were distributed as needed to the living quarters. The Harmonists constructed a new distillery, mills, stables, a brewery, and a tannery. In 1815, an impressive, wood-frame church and a tall clock tower were finished.

Back in Pennsylvania, the original Harmony community was experiencing hard times. Outsiders who had heard of the impending move stole into the town and made off with furniture, tools, and livestock. Then the state of Pennsylvania fined the community for refusing to provide volunteers for the state militia. (Father Rapp wanted his followers to be prepared for Christ's Second Coming, not outsiders' wars.) In May 1815, while fighting the fines in court as well as vandals on the town's streets, Frederick Rapp sold Harmony, Pennsylvania, to a local farmer and made preparations to move the remaining Harmonists to Indiana.

Over the next few years, Harmony, Indiana, flourished under Frederick Rapp's management. The society sold its products to buyers living as far away as Pittsburgh, Louisville, and St. Louis. With this success, the Harmony Society grew so wealthy that it was lending money to the young state of Indiana. Harmony's leaders also enjoyed the respect of the state's early legislatures. In 1816, Frederick Rapp was appointed a delegate to the Indiana Constitutional Convention, which wrote the new state's constitution. Four years later, he served on the committee choosing a site for the capital city.

But the Harmonists' prosperity came to an end when the market for their products declined. Suddenly, their German clothing, customs, and language made them the target of suspicion and ridicule among their neighbors. The society's leaders planned yet another move. In May 1824, the Harmonists began returning to western Pennsylvania. There they founded the town of Economy along the Ohio River, a little less than 20 miles northwest of Pittsburgh. Meanwhile, Father Rapp and Frederick Rapp sold Harmony, Indiana, to Robert Owen, a Scottish textile tycoon who planned to create his own utopian community on the site.

In Pennsylvania, the Harmonists were again successful at manufacturing and selling their goods. Wool and cotton mills were soon operating in Economy, along with a flour mill run by steam power, a new technology at that time. A store sold Economy's products to neighboring communities. To move their goods to distant markets, the Harmonists built their own wagons as well as their own steamboat, which Father Rapp named the *William Penn* after the man who had founded Pennsylvania as a haven for religious freedom almost 150 years before.

For several years, the people of Economy lived together peacefully, and Rapp's community seemed once again to be on solid footing. But in 1831, a stranger came

Quaker leader William Penn (1644-1718) founded Pennsylvania because he wanted a safe place for Quakers to live and worship.

This magnificent garden, known as the Great House Garden, was cultivated behind George Rapp's house in Economy, Pennsylvania.

who turned the utopia into a battleground. Bernhard Mueller, using the name Count Maximillian de Leon, moved to Economy to steal away some of the Harmonists to start his own utopia. Claiming to be a prophet, he began preaching the benefits of the outside world, such as marriage. Mueller's tirades made some of the Harmonists dissatisfied with the society's strict doctrines and with Father Rapp. But when the Harmonists held a vote in March 1832, members declared their loyalty to Rapp by a two-to-one margin.

After that vote, Mueller and his 250 followers agreed to leave Economy and move to the nearby town of Phillipsburg (now Monaca). The former Harmonists negotiated a settlement of $105,000 for their property. After the Muellerites squandered the payment, they decided to seize more money from Economy by force.

Father Rapp heard about the plans for Mueller's attack and prepared a defense. A Harmonist militia waited in the woods to ambush Mueller's men. Rapp and the Harmonists were ready when Mueller's followers marched on Economy and headed for the Great House. Before they could break in, they were pelted with stones

Mueller's militia threatened to loot Father Rapp's residence, the Great House (right). Economy's Feast Hall is shown on the left.

and bricks and doused with hot water thrown by Harmonist women from a window above the entrance. Fleeing the Great House, the Muellerites headed for the Economy hotel to steal valuables. But the Harmonist men emerged from the woods and drove the rioters from the hotel. With Economy secured, the Harmonists marched the Muellerites out of town to the accompaniment of a small band playing "The Rogue's March." Defeated, Mueller and his followers soon left the area for Louisiana, where Mueller died the next year.

Frederick Rapp's death in 1834 left the management of Economy to Father Rapp. The aging Rapp had little interest in business affairs, however, and entrusted the work to members Romelius Baker and Jacob Henrici. After Father Rapp died in 1847, seven other Harmony leaders were elected as superintendents with Baker and Henrici. Together, the nine-member Board of Elders oversaw Economy much as a modern-day corporate board runs a business. In addition to managing Economy's day-to-day operations, the board made investments in coal and railroad companies, developed western Pennsylvania oil deposits, and sold timber and coal from its properties. After the Civil War, the board of Economy acquired 900 acres of land on the banks of the Beaver River. They developed it into an industrial town called Beaver Falls by selling land to manufacturing companies.

As the Board of Elders and other members died off, the utopian Economy community gradually disappeared.

The discovery of oil in western Pennsylvania in 1859 launched a new industry and made a fortune for investors.

Even the name of the town was changed to Ambridge. With only a few members surviving, the Harmony Society formally dissolved itself in 1905, exactly 100 years after its founding. Ten years later, the state of Pennsylvania took over the town of Ambridge and preserved it as a historic site. Although his utopia had disappeared, Father Rapp remained a model for many twentieth-century visionaries who saw his combination of business success and religious vision as the key to building a successful utopia in the American wilderness.

A beehive adorns this portrait of British social reformer Robert Owen (1771-1858). Many utopians saw the beehive as a model of cooperative labor and communal living.

3

Robert Owen
New Harmony

On December 4, 1824, George Rapp, the leader of the Harmony Society, met with Robert Owen, a businessman and visionary from Scotland. Rapp wanted to sell Harmony's 30,000 acres of land and its buildings in the Indiana wilderness. He planned to move his remaining followers back to Pennsylvania, where he had founded his first Harmony community. There, Rapp hoped, the Harmonists could find new markets for many of the goods they had been producing in southwestern Indiana. Robert Owen wanted to start his own utopian experiment, so he was pleased to take the well-tilled fields and solid build-ings off Rapp's hands.

Robert Owen was born in 1771 in Newtown, Montgomeryshire (now in the county of Powys), Wales. Although he was an excellent student, Robert left school at the age of 10 and went to London. There he became an apprentice to a textile merchant. Robert was bright and resourceful and he quickly moved up. At age 18, the former laborer became part owner of his first business, which manufactured cotton-processing machines.

In his late twenties, Owen went to New Lanark, Scotland, where he had acquired partial ownership of a large cotton mill. That mill would make him a wealthy man. New Lanark was not only a profitable enterprise, it was also one of the world's first self-contained company towns. The town's housing and public buildings were built expressly for the use of the employees. The employ-ees, however, remained unhappy and inefficient. Owen saw New Lanark as a way to test his belief that human beings were shaped solely by their environment and by the conditions they experienced while growing up.

Owen used innovative methods at New Lanark—methods that would earn him a reputation as a radical social reformer. He reduced the long work days and raised the minimum working age of employees. Even when the company was experiencing hard times, he never cut workers' wages. A strong believer in public education, Owen also set up a school for the children of New Lanark

A visitor to Owen's New Lanark, Scotland, company town said he had never seen "a manufacturing community in which so much order, good government, tranquility, and rational happiness prevail."

employees, where new ideas in education could be tested and perfected. Students at the New Lanark school followed a course suited to their own abilities and interests, and ordinary book learning was delayed until students expressed an interest in it. Owen favored removing children from their parents as soon as possible and educating the young students in an environment in which experts and scientists used the latest methods to guide them.

Owen gained notoriety for his strong opposition to religion and established churches. Not only did he view religion as foolish and superstitious, he also saw churches as harmful and backward institutions that prevented humans from developing their abilities. Instead of promising heaven to hard workers, Owen substituted a scientific method for rewarding his laborers' production. A color-coded device Owen called a "silent monitor" graded employees on their efficiency and enthusiasm. The device had four faces: black for laziness, blue for minimal effort, yellow for diligence, and white for excellence. A superintendent handled the device and turned the faces according to each worker's attitude and productivity. The simple silent monitor proved effective. Owen's theory that humans were shaped solely by their environment was also proving accurate. The New Lanark workers—now with a better education and improved working conditions—were happier and more productive.

Confident that everyone would eventually agree with his theories, Owen publicized his methods in articles and speeches. He sought to convert educators, government officials, business owners, and the general public. In 1814, he wrote *New View of Society*, a book that explained his belief that people were products of their environment. Owen described the ideal conditions under which workers could live in the future in an 1817 letter to a London newspaper. If his methods were instituted, he predicted in the letter, "unity and mutual co-operation will become easy of execution, and the common practice of all."

But British society at the time was firmly set in its conservative ways. Although Owen's radical theories gained widespread interest, few people tried to put them into practice. Restless and impatient, he turned his attention to the United States—a land of opportunity for new ideas and new communities.

Owen had known about George Rapp and the Harmonists since 1815 and had once written to Rapp asking for details about his communities in Pennsylvania and Indiana. When he heard that Rapp wanted to sell the Harmony community in Indiana, Owen sailed with his son William to America in late 1824 to strike a deal. Owen's eldest son, Robert Dale Owen, was left to run the factory at New Lanark. Robert Owen admired the orderly streets and fields at Harmony and quickly agreed to purchase the land and buildings. Leaving William behind in charge, Owen left Indiana for the East Coast to promote a new version of Harmony (now called New Harmony) that would rise on the site of Rapp's village.

Robert Owen spoke twice before the U.S. Congress and gave lectures to the public in New York, Philadelphia, and other large cities. Soon everyone was talking about his newest social experiment. He gained the attention of congressmen and of President James Monroe, to whom he unveiled a six-foot scale model of the future New Harmony *phalanstery*. This elaborate structure was based on the phalanstery proposed by Charles Fourier, a French utopian thinker. Fourier had conceived of the phalanstery as a self-sufficient, independent city contained within a single large building. As Owen described it, the New Harmony phalanstery would provide all the space needed

In Robert Owen's vision, the phalanstery would not only house New Harmony, but would also serve as a utopian model for the rest of the world.

for the community's housing, employment, education, and recreation.

The phalanstery, Owen was convinced, would end the problems of cramped and unsanitary housing suffered by working-class families in manufacturing towns and large cities all over the world. Its walls would extend 1,000 feet on each side around a large central courtyard. The corners of the building would hold classrooms, libraries, lecture halls, and community dining halls. In the lower two floors of the long sides, there would be apartments for married couples. Single residents and children (who would live separately from their parents after reaching the age of two) would occupy the third story. Owen believed that the phalanstery's design would help to create an efficient egalitarian community in which members could become intellectually advanced people as well as productive workers. Eventually, more phalansteries would be built in other locations, and a network of Owenite communities would spread across North America and throughout the world.

Owen made an open invitation to all when promoting New Harmony, and hundreds flocked there. Under the direction of the inexperienced and unprepared William Owen, they moved into the leftover Harmonist housing. Many of the newcomers were unskilled laborers seeking to find the same kind of workers' utopia that Owen had created at New Lanark. Others were poor farmers envious of the prosperity enjoyed by Father Rapp's Harmonists. There were also idealists seeking to escape the competition of the everyday world and a few lazy people who simply wanted to live as easily as possible. Soon the town was overcrowded and chaotic.

William Owen must have breathed a sigh of relief when his father returned several months later, on April 13, 1825. Robert Owen, after all, had overseen every detail of New Lanark's industry and daily life. So it was he who could make New Harmony a smoothly running utopia.

After giving several speeches, Robert Owen decided to draft a constitution and move the town into its first stage, which he called the Preliminary Society. Members would have to bring their own tools and invest their own money in the town. Owen would sell or lease property to them and appoint a management committee to run the community's affairs. Residents were to perform the labor that best suited them. In return for their work, they would receive credits to buy food and household goods. The constitution provided some direction, but it unfortunately lacked detailed policies or procedures.

Robert Owen seemed to be more interested in promoting his vision than in seeing it through to completion. After announcing the Preliminary Society, he immediately left New Harmony again for promotional tours on the East Coast and in Europe. Then he went to Scotland, where he sold New Lanark to help pay off more of New Harmony's debt. Once again, William was left to contend with the expanding town and its growing problems.

While Robert Owen was away, New Harmony's overcrowding became intolerable. Bitter arguments broke out over housing in the former Harmonist dormitories, where families were sharing quarters until New Harmony's phalanstery was built. The neat fields, shops, and factories that New Harmony had inherited quickly deteriorated. Pigs ran loose in the streets, and weeds covered the vegetable gardens. Due to the lack of skilled labor, the mills, bakeries, brewery, and blacksmith shop shut down. A few small industries managed to survive, but they did not bring much money into the community.

Robert Owen returned to New Harmony with his son Robert Dale Owen and the "Boatload of Knowledge" in January 1826. The so-called Boatload of Knowledge was a group of intellectuals (who arrived by boat from Pittsburgh) Owen had recruited to come back with him to New Harmony, including distinguished geologist and educator William Maclure. Maclure was to head the school at New Harmony, which would be modeled after New Lanark's school. It would emphasize scientific subjects and skilled training in trades such as carpentry and masonry. Students would live in large dormitories apart from their parents, who would be allowed to see them only twice a year.

Either through blind optimism or a lack of patience, Owen made a speech proclaiming the town ready to progress from stage one (the Preliminary Society) to stage

William Maclure, pictured here, based his system of education on the theories of Swiss education reformer Johann Heinrich Pestalozzi. In Pestalozzian education, a child's individuality guided learning.

two. On February 5, 1826, a new constitution was adopted, and the town became known as the New Harmony Community of Equality. New Harmony would be based on communal ownership of property, equality of rights and duties, and freedom of speech. The constitution created six departments: agriculture; manufactures and mechanics; domestic economy; general economy; commerce; and literature, science, and education. Instead of Robert or William Owen, seven members elected to an executive council—with one representative from each department plus a secretary—would be responsible for the town's operations.

Unfortunately, the new constitution worked no better than the old one. Once again, Owen's plan did not go into the details of day-to-day management, and members of the executive council squabbled over their duties and powers. As a result, living conditions became even worse. This new constitution lasted less than two weeks before the council asked Owen to preside again over New Harmony. Robert Owen was back at the helm.

But Owen had been losing money on the community. He began selling off large parcels of land in order to meet the payments on his original purchase. His hoped-for phalanstery remained nothing more than a small-scale model. Meanwhile, the people of New Harmony began dividing into rival factions.

Perhaps just hoping to keep up the community's morale, Robert Owen delivered a Declaration of Mental

Overcrowded and in disarray, New Harmony was still picturesque in this painting by Karl Bodmer.

Independence on the Fourth of July, 1826. Although his followers were still feuding over housing and other matters, he declared that the members of New Harmony had now been freed of the two great evils afflicting mankind: private property and absurd systems of religion.

The declaration, however, did not improve conditions at New Harmony. By that autumn—less than two years after New Harmony's much-heralded opening—a steady stream of disillusioned residents was leaving. Rapidly growing poorer, Owen gave up his legal title to the town in January 1827, offering to lease it to anybody who would establish a new community founded on his ideas. Instead, residents began buying property directly, and the town slowly divided into private lots. William Maclure helped Owen pay his debts in return for a parcel of land. He established a school for orphans there.

On May 26, 1827, Owen made a farewell speech to his followers in New Harmony. He sailed for England six days later, leaving his remaining property in the care of his sons, who continued to sell off the town's buildings and land. New Harmony eventually became an ordinary town in Indiana, and its residents pursued occupations in agriculture and industry.

As his sons settled the tangled business affairs of New Harmony, Robert Owen traveled the world, still propounding his vision of the perfect egalitarian society. Owen spoke at workingmen's associations in England during their drive to establish the first trade unions, and he tried unsuccessfully to establish a government-funded utopia in Mexico.

Although Owen's phalanstery was never built and his community lasted just two and one-half years, his ideas and speeches did inspire several utopian experiments in Indiana, Illinois, Ohio, New York, and Pennsylvania during the next two decades. Robert Dale Owen left New Harmony in 1827 to build his own utopia at Nashoba, Tennessee. Believing that his father should not have welcomed the general public, the younger Owen gathered a more intellectual class of people to live in Nashoba. He sent novelist Fanny Wright, a close friend, to England to

Robert Dale Owen (1801–1877), shown here in 1875, served in the Indiana legislature and the U.S. Congress. He also helped to found the Smithsonian Institution in Washington, D.C.

recruit leading writers and thinkers to his community. But he quickly found that intellectuals made poor pioneers in the Tennessee wilderness, and the Nashoba colony failed even faster than New Harmony had.

The elder Owen, a long-time atheist, found religion in his later years. He also became fascinated with *spiritualism*, or communication with the dead. Owen came to the conclusion, in fact, that the lack of religion had handicapped his utopian experiment. Despite New Harmony's failure, Robert Owen remained popular among social reformers in both Great Britain and the United States until long after his death in 1858.

*No picture of Christian Metz exists, but the villages
of the Amana Colonies, including Amana, shown here
in about 1900, are monuments to his vision.*

4

Christian Metz
The Amana Colonies

*I*n the early sixteenth century, Martin Luther's anger over the power and corruption of the Roman Catholic Church brought about the Protestant Reformation. Luther and his followers hoped to deliver religion back into the hands of the common people. Christians would have a more personal and direct relationship with God, they believed, without the guidance of Catholic priests, bishops, or the pope. The Reformation eventually gave birth to all of the Protestant denominations, including the Lutheran Church. As it spread throughout what is

A Roman Catholic cathedral in Münster, Germany. The Catholic Church's alliances with European monarchs in the Middle Ages allowed it to amass great wealth even when most of its parishioners were desperately poor.

now Germany and northern Europe, Lutheranism became a powerful religious institution.

By the eighteenth century, however, many German believers were questioning Lutheranism. The church had grown quite large, and its complex theology and strict doctrines distanced it from many of its parishioners. As in the sixteenth century, people were searching for a more immediate and emotional religious experience. Many were seeking the signs, miracles, and direct relationship with God that had inspired the first Christian apostles.

The Pietist movement had begun in the late 1600s, with small groups meeting regularly to read the Bible, pray, and sing hymns. From Pietism came several other smaller groups. In 1714, two Pietists named Eberhard Ludwig Gruber and Johann Friedrich Rock founded a new sect called the Inspirationists.

The Inspirationists believed that God still spoke directly to Christians through signs and visions. To make his teachings clear, God also used certain selected individuals—known as "Instruments"—to communicate to the faithful. In their moments of inspiration, these people could directly convey the word of God.

Several small Inspirationist sects appeared in the Württemburg area in the eighteenth century, but most soon disbanded. The sect remained only a small branch of the Pietist movement until 1819, when a 24-year-old carpenter named Christian Metz became inspired. He began to wander throughout Germany, falling into trances and delivering sermons and messages as an Instrument.

Metz was not the sole leader of the True Inspiration Congregations, as the group came to call itself. A young servant named Barbara Heinemann also became an Instrument. But in 1823, Heinemann went against Inspirationist belief by marrying. Although she remained in the Inspirationist community, she lost influence and standing among her followers.

For defying the Lutheran Church, the group earned enemies among powerful church officials. Inspirationists also suffered arrests and imprisonment for refusing to send their children into the army since military service was required of all citizens. In 1842, after many years of persecution, Metz received the most important divine message of his life: he was told that the members of the True Inspiration Congregations must gather together and leave Germany.

Later that year, Metz sailed for the United States with four companions. The group landed in New York City and soon traveled to upstate New York. In this region, where the newly built Erie Canal was attracting new industries and settlement, many other groups had already established small communities to pursue their own dreams of social or religious utopia. Upstate New York was such a center of fiery spiritual fervor that the area was also known as the "Burned-Over District."

On what had once been a Seneca Indian reservation near the rapidly growing city of Buffalo, Metz and the Inspirationists bought 5,000 acres of land. They began clearing trees and raising cabins on this tract. As soon as the new homes were ready, Metz summoned the rest of the congregation to follow him across the Atlantic Ocean. Metz's followers sold all their goods and land, pooled their money, and began arriving early in 1843. By the end of the year, more than 1,000 Inspirationists were living in the newly built town of Eben-Ezer.

Under Metz's guidance, the Inspirationists built the villages of Upper, Middle, and Lower Eben-Ezer. Each had its own school, stores, workshops, and meeting hall. Every large house on the streets was home to several families. The skilled factory workers and farmers who had joined the Inspirationists were soon producing goods for growing markets in Buffalo and other upstate towns.

The Inspirationists grew prosperous. But the rapid growth of the surrounding region caused land prices to rise, making it difficult for the community to expand. So Metz and his followers began looking west, where good farmland was still available for a low price.

In 1854, a group from Eben-Ezer traveled to the Iowa River valley, about 75 miles west of the Mississippi River. There they found deposits of limestone and stands of good timber, as well as fertile soil. And the land was cheap. After purchasing 3,000 acres, the group sent for the rest of the Inspirationists. Over the next 10 years, the members of the congregation gradually sold their land in Eben-Ezer and moved west to Iowa.

The Inspirationists named their new community Amana after a hill mentioned in the Bible's Song of Songs: "Come with me from Lebanon, my spouse," wrote the Bridegroom. "Look from the top of Amana." Following the model of Eben-Ezer, the members built several new towns. As each village was completed, a group would arrive from New York to take up residence. The villages were named Amana, East Amana, Middle Amana, West Amana, South Amana, and Amana near the Hill. The Inspirationists also bought the small town of Homestead,

Smokestacks of factories rise in the distance behind the houses of Amana's residents. Townspeople's homes faced away from the streets, and fences protected yards from the cattle that were run through the town.

which was located on the Rock Island Railroad line. They would use the railroad to ship goods to their markets in the East and the Midwest.

At first, the Amana villages were each arrayed along a long street, with farm buildings at one end and factories and workshops at the other end. Each town had its own blacksmith and woodworking shops, as well as a school and a meeting hall. Fire wardens watched over the town from the tops of towers built along the main streets. There were inns for visitors or travelers who happened to pass through. As in Eben-Ezer, families shared homes. The community also built housing for laborers they hired from the surrounding farms and small towns.

A board of 13 trustees was elected to oversee the Amana Society, as the group was now called. The board then appointed six elders to oversee each town since the towns operated independently. Factory foremen chosen by the trustees managed the society's industries, such as sawmills, woolen mills, and grist mills. The mills and factories were spread around the community. West Amana had a grist mill, for example, and Amana near the

The Amana people honored the skill and hard work of craftsmen such as blacksmiths, whose expertise was handed down from master to apprentice.

*Amana's water-powered woolen mill. The Amana
Colonies are still famous for their fine woolen goods.*

Hill was home to a tannery and a sawmill. To provide
water power for the mills, the Inspirationists dug a six-
mile canal that diverted water from the Iowa River.

Although the Amana Society prospered, its members
lived simple, frugal lives. Their clothing was as plain as
possible to discourage frivolity and envy. Women were
forbidden to wear their hair loose, and they sat apart from
men at public meetings. Marriage was permitted, but
the elders had to approve each engagement, and all couples had to wait until the man reached the age of 24
before they could be married. Women could not marry

outside the community, but men were allowed to if their brides converted to Inspirationism. Otherwise, the couple had to leave Amana.

Amana Society schools educated children between the ages of 6 and 13. In addition to ordinary study, all students had to knit gloves, scarves, and other articles. The community leaders believed this would help them form good work habits and avoid useless play and troublemaking in the streets outside the school. After finishing their

In addition to reading, writing, and arithmetic, students in this class in Homestead learned the Bible, Inspirationist doctrine, and music.

Boys practicing knitting. The gloves and socks they made were sold to customers in Iowa and New York.

schooling, children began an apprenticeship in one of the workshops or factories to learn a trade.

Supplies were distributed to each town according to the needs of its members. Each member received a small annual allowance for personal items: up to $100 for men, $40 for women, and $10 for children. Each purchase made by a member was recorded in an account book. At the end of the year, an accountant checked the entries. Any surplus money in a member's account could be carried over to the next year.

Members dined together in large community halls, where 40 or 50 men and women ate their meals in silence. Prayer meetings took place 11 times each week. Members who were considered Instruments delivered sermons, in which they warned the community against wrongdoing and guided members to the proper course of action in personal matters. At these meetings, Metz and the other Instruments often fell into a trance before delivering religious and practical instruction. A member carefully took down the inspired words uttered during meetings, and each year the Amana Society published a book of these sayings.

The community became less strict over time, but the Amana Society still tried to observe the 21 important doctrines in *Rules for Daily Life*, a work written in the 1720s by Eberhard Ludwig Gruber, one of the founders of the Inspirationists. His rules for living a pure Christian life included the following:

> VII. Do not disturb your serenity or peace of mind—hence neither desire nor grieve.
>
> XI. Be in all things sober, without levity or laughter; and without vain and idle words, works, or thoughts; much less heedless or idle.
>
> XVI. Have no intercourse with worldly-minded men; never seek their society; speak little with them, and never without need; and then not without fear and trembling.
>
> XVIII. Fly from the society of women-kind as much as possible, as a very highly dangerous magnet and magical fire.
>
> XX. Dinners, weddings, feasts, avoid entirely; at the best there is sin.

The meeting house in Homestead. The entire community came on Saturdays for services, and people met in smaller groups every evening and three mornings each week for prayer and Bible reading.

Metz warned his followers to lead a life of serenity and sincerity. There was to be no criticism of others, no selfishness, and no striving for material goods or comfort. Members were to bear any suffering in silence and always were to remain sober and calm. Laughter was frowned upon, and contact with the outside world was discouraged.

The Amanans celebrated few holidays. The most important celebration, which they called the Lord's Supper, lasted several days and took place whenever Metz was inspired to hold it. On these occasions, the congregation celebrated the biblical Last Supper, in which Christ broke bread with his disciples just before his arrest and crucifixion. The Lord's Supper at the Amana Society included a meal of bread, cake, chocolate, and wine.

During the celebration, as a scribe wrote down their words, Metz and other Instruments would give divinely inspired sermons, messages, and warnings.

Once each year, members met to confess their sins publicly to their elders, to resolve any disputes, and to place their spiritual condition under the close examination of the Instruments. To measure their spiritual attainment, the Amanans divided themselves into three orders. Children, married couples, and new members were in the low order; ordinary members were in the middle order; those who had lived in the community the longest and had demonstrated the most commitment to Amana's ideals belonged to the highest order. Members who had displeased the elders or the Instruments could fall in the Amana hierarchy. Others showing religious inspiration or strong devotion to the group could rise.

In all the years she had lived in the Amana Society, Barbara Heinemann had remained loyal to the group and its ideals. After the death of Christian Metz in 1867, Heinemann became the community's spiritual leader. Under her leadership, the colonies grew to their highest population in the 1870s and 1880s. After her death in 1883, however, older members died off and most of the children of the Amana Society left the community.

Losing membership, the Amana Society faced the prospect of disbanding. Instead, the remaining members decided in 1932 to turn the community into a corporation, which they would still call the Amana Society. The

The Inspirationists of Amana in the 1920s still lived as they had for almost a century, in neat, unpainted houses of equal size. The whole community gathered in dining halls for meals.

community's property was sold to members, who also received shares of Amana Society stock in proportion to the amount of time they had lived in the group.

In place of a religious utopia, Amana became a production cooperative, with members working together to make and market their goods. In the factories, assembly lines were set up and modern production equipment was used. In 1933, the Amana communities built a new high school, in which English replaced German as the language of instruction. Members were permitted to marry freely outside the community, and the strict rules for religious observance and daily life were left behind.

Business grew steadily for Amana. One of its most prosperous divisions, Amana Refrigeration (now Amana Appliances), became widely known for kitchen products and appliances. In 1950, the Amana Society sold Amana Refrigeration. The Amana Society still includes a church organization, divided into seven congregations—one for each of the towns of the original Amana Society. Now called the Amana Colonies, the quiet and orderly villages of Christian Metz's utopia have become Iowa's most popular tourist attraction.

Entertainer Bob Hope promotes an Amana refrigerator in the 1940s. Founded in Amana in 1934, Amana Refrigeration became one of the nation's leading makers of kitchen appliances.

*An intellectual who loved the city, George Ripley
(1802-1880) found the same passion for farming as
he had for literature. At Brook Farm, he tried to
create a community of book-loving laborers.*

5

George Ripley
Brook Farm

*I*n September 1836, a group of men and women gathered in Boston, Massachusetts, for the first meeting of the Transcendental Club. They came to discuss art, religion, politics, and the latest works of the novelists, historians, and philosophers of the day. Ralph Waldo Emerson, Henry David Thoreau, Nathaniel Hawthorne, and other members of the club disagreed on many things, but they did hold a few beliefs in common. All believed in the power of ideas to improve the world. They also wanted to change the competitive and sometimes violent society

Henry David Thoreau (1817-1862) did more than talk about improving the world. In the 1840s, he experimented with living simply and independently in the woods. He described this attempt in his famous 1854 book, Walden.

they lived in, which seemed to ignore philosophy and art in the pursuit of money, status, and power.

The Transcendentalists thought that people could solve their problems without the guidance of organized religion. "A man contains all that is needful . . . within himself," Emerson once wrote in his diary. Good and evil exist only within the individual conscience, he taught, and each person must find an individual philosophy of living. "The highest revelation," according to Emerson, "is that God is in every man." Influenced by Buddhist philosophy and mysticism, the Transcendentalists also believed in following intuition and inspiration, which came in moments of "transcendence," rather than from religious doctrines or scientific theories. If everyone learned from transcendental intuition, society would change for the better. No one needed politicians, preachers, and other authority figures to lay down rules or show others the way.

Emerson and several of the other members of the Transcendental Club came from the Unitarian ministry. One of them was an ambitious 34-year-old preacher named George Ripley. Ripley had graduated from Harvard Divinity School in 1826 and served as minister of a Unitarian church in Boston. Unitarians welcomed many ideas from other religious groups, but they opposed the strict teachings of traditional Calvinists, who believed that a person's fate in heaven or hell was predestined.

The Calvinist movement began in the sixteenth century under John Calvin and influenced the development of other religious groups, such as the Congregationalists and the Puritans, both of which had been influential in New England since the colonial period. Although the Unitarian Church had also been founded in the 1500s in Europe, most Unitarians in nineteenth-century America were people who had left the Congregational Church. Unitarianism set itself apart from most Christian groups by denying the doctrine of the *Trinity*, the belief that God exists in three forms: God, Jesus Christ, and the Holy Spirit. In mid-nineteenth-century New England, Ripley and other Unitarians had come to believe in a kindly God who helped humans achieve perfection. Unitarian and

Calvinist ministers battled in the city's pulpits, with Ripley preaching to members of his congregation that good works on earth would make them worthy in God's eyes. But he grew frustrated that most people were unable to carry this Christian ideal into their everyday lives.

George Ripley, who was one of the original participants at the Transcendental Club meetings, recognized in the Transcendentalists the same inability to act. It seemed that while they loved to talk and dream up clever solutions to the world's problems, they never bothered to put any of their ideas into action. If Transcendentalist ideas were not applied to the problems of American society, Ripley wondered, what good were they?

Ripley had worked out his own personal philosophy. The fulfilled person, he concluded, was one who took part in both the intellectual and the laboring world. A small community of such people, sharing their individual skills and their personal philosophies, could become self-supporting and also gain a deeper understanding of the world. They might even succeed in creating their own ideal society.

While pondering his ideas, Ripley spent the summer of 1840 at a rented farmhouse in the town of West Roxbury, near Boston. There he and his wife, Sophia, enjoyed strolling through 170 acres of beautiful forests, lovely meadows, and peaceful pastures. A small stream ran through the farm and gave the place its name—Brook Farm.

Here was the perfect spot, Ripley decided, to carry out his utopian ideal—a small community of enlightened laborers. A self-supporting group could come to Brook Farm and leave behind the strife of a competitive capitalist economy. Everyone would work according to his or her abilities and share the fruits of common labor and knowledge. A school would instruct the children of members in standard subjects as well as in Transcendentalist and utopian ideals. Adult members of the group would study the world's philosophies and begin to form their own new philosophies. If it succeeded, Ripley believed, Brook Farm would provide a model for a better society in the future. He left his church later that year and prepared to start his community.

Even before paying for the land and the buildings or writing any constitution to govern their new community, George and Sophia Ripley moved into Brook Farm in the spring of 1841 along with 15 other people. Two farmers in the group, William Allen and Frank Farley, made arrangements to buy a small herd of livestock. George's sister Marianne Ripley and ministers George Bradford and Warren Burton were also among the first Brook Farm residents. Nathaniel Hawthorne, who would immortalize this attempt at utopian living in his book *The Blithedale Romance*, arrived later that spring after leaving his job at the Boston Customs House. Of the group, only Allen and Farley had any experience with farming or manual labor, but the members of the new community were eager to try.

Ripley did not have enough money of his own to buy the property. To raise funds, he borrowed money and organized a joint-stock corporation. He asked friends and Transcendentalist supporters to buy shares of stock in the community, guaranteeing 5 percent annual interest on each $500 share. All stockholders would be members of Brook Farm and entitled to vote on how the money should be spent. Stockholders would also receive free tuition for their children to attend the Brook Farm school.

After the new members worked hard all summer on the farm, Ripley decided it was time to purchase the land and draft a constitution so they could start their community. He sold a total of 24 shares of stock to 10 different people. Ripley himself bought 3 shares, and Nathaniel Hawthorne bought 2. But Ralph Waldo Emerson, one of the most famous writers of the day, decided that his money was probably safer in the bank.

On October 11, 1841, Ripley paid $10,500 for the farm and drew up the Articles of Association, his formal plan for how the Brook Farm Association would operate. Members paid for room and board with their labor. Those who chose not to work could instead pay $4 a week—about the going rate in Boston then—for their lodging and meals. To keep out undesirables, Ripley decreed in the Articles of Association that each new member must go through a two-month probation period. At the end of this time, the current members would vote, with two-thirds approval needed for acceptance.

At first, Brook Farm members went about creating their utopia with light-hearted enthusiasm. After performing their manual labor, members found plenty of time for picnics and boating parties. At night, they enjoyed lectures, music, and dancing. Reading clubs were formed, and discussion groups debated different topics every night. The Amusement Group was formed to stage plays for the Brook Farm members and their neighbors in West Roxbury.

The members gave each building at Brook Farm a nickname that reminded them of the country setting of their new life. The main farmhouse became the Hive, while the school across the road was known as the Nest. The community raised new living quarters and named them the Aerie, the Cottage, and the Pilgrim House.

Ripley figured that it would be a while before Brook Farm was entirely self-supporting. In the meantime, the community's income would have to come from the sale of its food and goods, shares bought by new members, lodging fees paid by the nonworking members, and tuition paid by nonmembers for the Brook Farm school.

Brook Farm was best known for its school, and the Ripleys attached great importance to the institution. Most of the time, the school was also Brook Farm's only reliable source of income. Under Sophia's supervision, an elementary school taught children from 6 to 10 years of age. A six-year college-preparatory course offered botany, mathematics, Latin, German, literature, and philosophy.

The Brook Farm school, known as the Nest, and the Hive (the two buildings on the right) were already built before George Ripley and the others moved there. From left to right, the Pilgrim House, the Cottage, and the Aerie were constructed during the next few years.

School was not conducted in the traditional sense, however. Teachers and students decided when and where to have classes. Instead of lecturing, teachers held open discussions with students. The school enjoyed such a good reputation that it drew students from other states and even foreign countries.

During the 1840s, people were fascinated by utopian experiments, and many leading thinkers, journalists, social reformers, and educators took an interest in Brook Farm. Horace Greeley, editor of the *New York Tribune* newspaper, became an enthusiastic supporter. Ralph Waldo Emerson dropped in several times, as did Margaret Fuller, who edited the *Dial*, the Transcendentalist literary journal. Visiting Brook Farm became fashionable for the Boston area's writers and intellectuals.

Brook Farm had widespread interest and support, but it was not financially successful. Skilled farm labor was in short supply, and the community's philosophers soon lost interest in the hard work of farming, building homes, and making necessary repairs. The land was picturesque, but the soil was poor and did not produce enough surplus crops for sale. Products of the Brook Farm workshops, such as window frames and shoes, found

In Brook Farm's first years, Margaret Fuller (1810-1850) was working on a pioneering feminist work, Woman in the Nineteenth Century *(1845). She gave lectures at Brook Farm about her ideas.*

a limited market. Few new members joined, and the community attracted no new investors. By 1843, Brook Farm faced mounting debt. Growing disillusioned with manual labor and the impracticality of Ripley's utopia, Nathaniel Hawthorne and other members were leaving Brook Farm.

Feeling the community needed better organization and direction, Ripley turned to Albert Brisbane, who headed the Charles Fourier Society of New York. From Brisbane, Ripley learned about Charles Fourier, a French

Charles Fourier (1772-1837), left, and Albert Brisbane (1809-1890). Brisbane studied with Fourier in Paris and was responsible for introducing his ideas in the United States.

philosopher and social reformer. Unhappy with the competitive world he lived in, Fourier had designed a complex and tightly structured utopian society. According to Fourier's plan, human society would organize itself into joint-stock companies, like Brook Farm, called *phalanxes*. Each phalanx would include between 1,620 and 1,800 members who would share meals and live together in large housing complexes known as phalansteries. Also like Brook Farm, individuals would perform the jobs for which they were best suited.

In a phalanx, labor would be divided into a highly regimented system of "groups" and "series." Several people in the phalanx would work together at a particular task to form a group. Groups that performed similar tasks made up a series. Every possible task was categorized and assigned to a group in a series. For example, a phalanx would have a farming series that included a group of people who planted seeds. The people who weeded and harvested the plants were in different groups in the same farming series. To prevent monotony in Fourier's system, a member was encouraged to work in many different groups and even in different series. This system, Fourier and Brisbane believed, would guarantee community harmony and individual well-being.

Brisbane enthusiastically took up Fourier's ideas in his 1840 book, *The Social Destiny of Man*, which inspired the establishment of several phalanxes in North America. One of Brisbane's most influential allies was Horace

Greeley, whose *New York Tribune* newspaper featured prominent articles on Fourierism. Because Europeans were slow to experiment with Fourier's ideas, Brisbane believed that the United States provided the most promising ground for attempting Fourier's utopia.

Ripley was converted, but many other Brook Farm members, including Charles Dana, one of its most prominent teachers, were not. They were skeptical of Fourier's regimented plan and felt Brook Farm would lose its emphasis on education and its many recreational activities if Fourierism was adopted. Ripley prevailed, however, and the directors of the Brook Farm Association passed a second constitution in January 1844. Immediately, members began to reorganize Brook Farm into the Fourierist Brook Farm Phalanx.

To direct the production of goods, the Department of Industry was established with three main Fourierist series: agricultural, mechanical, and domestic. Each series had a chief, a position that was up for election every two months. In the agricultural series were groups such as weeding, planting, milking, and hoeing. The domestic series had kitchen, ironing, and washing groups. A teaching group was organized at the Brook Farm school, and a miscellaneous group carried out odd jobs. Brook Farm even had a group, the Sacred Legion, for the most undesirable tasks. The Sacred Legion took on duties such as butchering hogs and digging ditches. Members of Brook Farm chose the groups to which they would devote most of their time and labor. But just as with Fourier's plan, they could jump from one area of work to another for the sake of variety.

Brook Farm's conversion to Fourierism sparked some renewed interest in Ripley's utopia. New residents moved to the Brook Farm Phalanx, but many old members left the community. Despite his opposition to the change, Charles Dana did decide to remain an active member at Brook Farm. In 1845, Brook Farm took out a loan to cover the cost of building a large phalanstery to house all of the community's members. Carpenters and masons worked through the winter, and the building was near completion by early 1846. But on the night of March 3, while the members of the Brook Farm Phalanx held a celebration to mark the end of the long, expensive, and difficult project, the phalanstery caught on fire and burned to the ground.

The Brook Farm Phalanx had not yet insured the building, so the utopia suffered a devastating financial loss from which it could not recover. Unable to borrow more money, the community prepared to rent out its remaining buildings, and most members left the Brook Farm Phalanx. In August 1847, a board of trustees that included some of the original Brook Farm shareholders took possession of the property. They prepared to sell it off to begin paying Brook Farm's many debts. In 1849, the farm was sold to the town of Roxbury at an auction. Roxbury established a homeless shelter in the buildings.

*The town of Roxbury (now part of Boston), shown in
1850. Roxbury operated its shelter for only a year
before the Hive and the Nest burned to the ground.*

Brook Farm had been one of three Fourierist pha-
lanxes operating in the United States. The six-year-old
Ceresco Phalanx in Wisconsin folded the same year as
Brook Farm. The North American Phalanx in New
Jersey, which had been founded in 1843, lasted until 1854.

After Brook Farm's sale, George and Sophia Ripley
moved to New York, where they continued to print the
Brook Farm journal, the *Harbinger*. Burdened with debts,
Ripley was forced to sell his most important possession,
his personal library. Within two years, the *Harbinger* had
ceased production, and Ripley took a journalist's job at
Horace Greeley's *New York Tribune*.

Even though Ripley was no longer involved in utopian projects, he continued to make important contributions to American literature and culture. In 1862, a year after the death of his wife, he helped to write and produce the *American Cyclopedia*, a collection of articles on American society. By the time of George Ripley's death in 1880, however, Transcendentalism had given way to new philosophies, leaving behind a circle of renowned writers and the memory of a utopian experiment in the meadows of Brook Farm.

Horace Greeley (seated second from right) and the staff of the New York Tribune. *Charles Dana (standing in middle) edited the paper for years and supervised George Ripley (seated far right), who achieved distinction as the newspaper's book critic.*

John Humphrey Noyes (1811-1886) encouraged his followers to strive for heavenly perfection on earth. His Oneida community was one of the longest lasting and most controversial utopias of the nineteenth century.

6

John Humphrey Noyes
The Oneida Community

*T*he Protestant ministers of New England in the 1830s were taking sides in an intense battle. A single question lay at the heart of the struggle: Were humans wretched and wicked beings whose destinies were controlled by God alone? Or could people change their evil nature and attain salvation? Calvinist ministers believed that humans were sinful by nature and only God could save them from hell. Their sole chance at leading a virtuous life was to allow themselves to be guided by God's ministers. The Methodists and other, newer religious groups opposed this view. They believed men and women should allow their own consciences to guide them. People had a choice of whether or not to commit sins, these groups claimed, and some congregations even contended that a person could attain perfection in the eyes of God.

This conflict of ideas was fought fiercely in the old colonial city of New Haven on Connecticut's southern coast. Once the seat of the most strictly Calvinist colony in New England, New Haven saw several of its congregations convert to the new ideas and religions of the early nineteenth century. On the top of a wooded hill where the Yale Divinity School looked out over the city and its churches, a powerful revelation came to a divinity student. This revelation would inspire John Humphrey Noyes to build and lead one of the most successful—and notorious—utopian communities in history.

Noyes was born in Brattleboro, Vermont, in September 1811. His father was a successful shopkeeper who also served one term in the Vermont legislature. His mother was deeply religious and taught her eight children to study the New Testament to find their own religious paths. At the age of 15, John enrolled in Dartmouth College. The young man graduated four years later, in 1830. Uncertain about his future, Noyes worked for a short time in the law office of his brother-in-law.

In 1831, Noyes attended a Methodist revival that changed the course of his life. The preacher inspired the crowd to shout aloud their praise of God. He told them

John Wesley (1703-1791) was the leader of a group of Oxford College students in England who founded the Methodist Church. Methodists were known for their close study of the Bible and their belief that salvation could be attained through faith in God.

to question the religious doctrines they had been taught. Captivated, Noyes decided to join the ministry. He began at the Andover Theological Seminary before transferring to the Yale Divinity School in autumn 1832.

While still a student at Yale, Noyes began attending what was called a "free church" in New Haven, where new and sometimes radical ideas about Christianity were expressed. At this church, Noyes was drawn to a religious concept known as Perfectionism. Perfectionists argued that humans could reach a state of perfect love with God. Noyes, who recently had been ordained a minister, set out to earn perfection through countless hours of prayer and Bible study. He believed that the Second Coming of Christ had already occurred sometime around A.D. 70, making possible a heaven on earth. Humans, he argued, thus could work to achieve a state of perfection and attain salvation. On February 20, 1834, Noyes received the revelation that he had finally reached that state and was cleansed of all sin.

Noyes publicly announced that he was perfect, but the Yale Divinity School thought otherwise and expelled him for his beliefs. Under intense pressure from his fellow ministers at Yale, Noyes was also forced to give up his license to preach. Even members of the free church saw Noyes's claim as blasphemous. Although Noyes left New Haven in disgrace, he did not give up his convictions or stop preaching. For two years, he traveled throughout New England proclaiming his ideas. Then he returned to Putney, Vermont, in 1836 to establish his own following of Perfectionists near his hometown.

Noyes knew that most people would never accept his beliefs. To avoid persecution, he would have to establish his own church on his own land. In 1841, he took the first step in this direction by founding the Society for Inquiry. Then, Noyes and several of his siblings bought some property in Putney with $20,000 inherited from their father. The income from a store and two farms supported their small community, and all the members worked together and shared the products of their labor.

Over the next few years, a handful of people joined the Society for Inquiry.

During his years of listening to the radical ideas of the free church, Noyes had concluded that certain traditional moral principles were unimportant for those who had attained Perfection. Traditional marriage, he insisted, led to selfishness and jealousy. Much like the Shakers, Noyes believed that the institution of marriage did not exist in the afterlife, and, therefore, should not exist in the ideal society. But whereas the Shakers committed themselves to celibacy, Noyes came up with the concept of "complex marriage." In a complex marriage, all of the men would be married to all of the women. Everyone would freely exchange marriage partners and could express love to more than one person.

Despite his idea of complex marriage, Noyes had been married to a Perfectionist follower named Harriet Holton since 1838. Their marriage had been traditional thus far. Foreseeing that complex marriage could lead to unwanted pregnancies, Noyes decided to develop his own new form of birth control. He tested and perfected his method for two years and finally decided it was effective enough to use in complex marriage.

In 1846, John and Harriet Noyes entered into the first complex marriage with another Perfectionist couple. Soon other members of the community were also exchanging their husbands and wives. Rumors of the unusual marital arrangements reached outsiders in Putney, and it was not long before a local court charged Noyes with adultery.

Unwilling to face the charges and determined to carry out his Perfectionist utopia, Noyes looked for a solution. A number of people who belonged to a different Perfectionist sect had already started a small community near the town of Oneida, just east of the Finger Lakes region in upstate New York. When the Oneida group invited Noyes and the Society for Inquiry to join them, Noyes eagerly accepted. In the spring of 1848, a total of 45 adults and children moved from Putney to Oneida.

The Oneida community lived on an estate of 40 acres that once had been part of the Oneida Indian reservation. There was one frame house, an abandoned hut, and an old sawmill on the property. When Noyes officially established the Oneida Association, he invited Perfectionists scattered around the northeastern United States to join them.

The Perfectionists at Oneida contributed all their money and property to the community and received free room and board. Members built a large wooden house in which many of them lived. In the 1860s, they replaced this structure with an enormous brick structure, called the Mansion House, that served as a residence for the entire community.

Oneida was designed to be a self-supporting community. Members were assigned tasks that best suited their abilities and interests. To prevent monotony, the

Started in the 1860s, the grand Mansion House grew with numerous additions. It still stands today.

assignments usually lasted for only a year. Departments such as dentistry, laundry, carpentry, landscaping, printing, music, and repairs were established to manage the community's activities and provide for all its needs. Women stepped outside of the traditional setting of the kitchen to work in these areas alongside men. Heads of each department controlled the budget and received weekly reports from their workers. By virtue of their advanced state of Perfection, Noyes and a small circle of his followers, known as "central members," directed the community.

In the early years, the Oneida community struggled to survive on the meager income mainly provided from agriculture. As Noyes accepted skilled tradesmen into the group, however, Oneida became a center of several small-scale industries. A blacksmith shop, a mill, and a silk-weaving operation were started. Soon, the Oneidans were selling traveling bags, sewing kits, silk thread, and various household goods. Inventor Sewell Newhouse joined Oneida, bringing his patented design for a steel animal trap. Known for their high quality, the traps found a wide market, and the income from their sale rescued the community from financial hardship.

An advertisement for a Sewell Newhouse steel trap

Oneida women scandalized Americans by cutting their hair, wearing shorter dresses with bloomers, and working in traditionally male fields. This picture in Frank Leslie's Illustrated Newspaper *mocks the female bookkeepers at Oneida by depicting them flirting with male visitors.*

Another factor that contributed to Oneida's success was Noyes's practice of allowing young members to leave the community either to study or to work in factories. Several young men attended Yale and returned with expertise in medicine, engineering, and architecture. Both young men and women worked in factories outside Oneida and brought back designs for new machines and new methods of producing goods. Oneida became a community famous for its manufacturing.

As the Oneida community became more established, other smaller Perfectionist communities based on Noyes's beliefs were founded in Connecticut, New Jersey, and Brooklyn, New York. But most of these groups were unable to support themselves with farming or industry, and all but the one at Wallingford, Connecticut, were abandoned by 1855. Their members moved to either Oneida or Wallingford. Oneida would mainly focus on industry and Wallingford on agriculture. Together, the two settlements were home to about 300 men, women, and children.

Noyes carefully screened each outsider applying for membership. Every applicant was required to learn Perfectionist doctrine thoroughly during a year-long trial membership. After becoming a full member, the new Oneidans began at the bottom of the Perfectionist spiritual ladder, which Noyes called "ascending fellowship." Over the years, new applicants replaced those who left the community, and the population of Oneida held steady. Those who chose to leave were reimbursed for their original contribution. Even people who had brought nothing were given $100 and a new suit of clothes.

Because complex marriage was central to his concept of achieving perfection, Noyes presided with great care over the system of matrimony he had introduced at Putney. All members were in theory free to have what they called "interviews" with any member of the opposite sex, but no one was forced into sexual relations. A man made an application to a selected woman, who was free to accept or reject his offer. Eventually, Noyes decreed that invitations must be sent through a third party to avoid embarrassment and hurt feelings. The older members and those who showed the least discrimination in choosing partners were considered to be the most spiritually advanced on the Perfectionist scale of ascending fellowship. The highest spot was occupied by Noyes himself.

The Oneida community in about 1860. Noyes stands in the right foreground with clasped hands.

By the principle of ascending fellowship, less perfect Oneidans should aspire to pair with those who had attained a higher spiritual rank. This encouraged younger members to mate with those who were older and more experienced. The principle also was meant to prevent the younger members from falling into monogamous love affairs with each other, which was condemned as being selfish and contrary to Perfectionist beliefs. Such monogamous attachments were a common pitfall of complex marriage. When two people fell in love, one of them was sent to the Wallingford community, and the couple was kept apart until either their emotions cooled or they both left the Perfectionist society.

In order to reach perfection in God's eyes, the members of Oneida were taught to eliminate selfish desires and join wholeheartedly in the life of the community. There were few exclusive friendships, no private letters or conversations, and no diaries. When a member acted against the principles of Perfectionism, he or she could ask for a "mutual criticism," a concept introduced by Noyes. When undergoing a mutual criticism, the guilty member sat before others in the community who knew that member best. Noyes presided over the session, and he and the others would take turns stating frankly what was wrong— or, once in a while, right—with the person who asked for the criticism. Everyone in the community was encouraged to subject themselves to mutual criticisms except for Noyes, who was, of course, already perfect.

Despite the use of birth control, children were still born at Oneida. Noyes wanted spiritually advanced children instead of unplanned conceptions, so in the 1860s he began a program of selective breeding, which he called "stirpiculture." Noyes sought to produce offspring who would start life with a higher degree of spiritual attainment than that of ordinary infants. The members of the stirpiculture committee considered applications from hopeful mothers and fathers, and the selected parents were then paired off. As a result of the program, 58 children were born, 10 of them sons and daughters of Noyes. A wing of the Mansion House, known as the Children's House, provided a home and school for the "stirpicults," who, like other children accidentally born at Oneida, were separated from their parents and placed in a community nursery after weaning from nursing.

Oneida enjoyed years of success until the late 1870s, when rivalries began plaguing the community. Noyes was growing older and wanted to give his responsibilities to one of his sons. Even though the young man was not interested and the community objected to the change, Noyes insisted. Noyes also sought to give away some of his rights as the head of complex marriages. Noyes had always been the first marriage partner for a young girl, but now, in his old age, he occasionally appointed one of the central members to perform that duty instead.

In 1879, James Towner, a central member, questioned the leader's right to appoint the "first husband."

Since coming to Oneida in 1874, James Towner had risen to become a central member of the community. But by 1879, when he turned against Noyes, he had not yet been chosen to be a first husband to an Oneida girl.

Soon rival groups formed around the two men. Known as "Townerites" and "Noyesites," the two parties struggled for control of the community. While this strife continued, Oneida was coming under attack from people outside the community who threatened Noyes and his followers with lawsuits and criminal charges, including adultery and *statutory rape*, or sexual relations with a minor.

Noyes fled to Canada in June 1879 to avoid the threats, but he kept in touch with the community through letters. Realizing that complex marriage could eventually lead to serious legal troubles, he now urged the Oneidans to abandon the system. The members agreed and then arranged a total of 37 legal marriages among themselves. Oneidans still believed in Noyes's Perfectionist doctrines, but the founder's influence on the Oneida community would never again be the same.

In 1881, seeking to keep the community alive in some form, the members of Oneida transformed it into a corporation called the Oneida Community, Limited. The community divided up its property and issued shares worth $25 each to a total of 226 members. The number of shares received by each member was based on the duration of membership and the member's initial contribution. If members wished to stay at Mansion House, they now had to pay for their room and board. Children were allowed to remain at the Mansion House and continued to receive an education until the age of 16. At that age, they were given a cash payment of $200 to give them a start in the outside world.

By this time, Noyes had moved to the town of Clifton, on the Canadian side of Niagara Falls. (Towner and his followers, meanwhile, had moved far away to the town of Santa Ana, California.) A few of Noyes's oldest and closest followers joined him in Canada, where he would live out the remainder of his days. When John Humphrey Noyes died on April 13, 1886, the Oneidans arranged to have his body moved back to the United States for burial.

During the early 1890s, the aging directors of Oneida saw their business gradually lose customers to other manufacturers. But that changed in 1894 when Pierrepont Burt Noyes, a stirpiculture son of John

Not only did Pierrepont Noyes rescue the company from financial ruin, he also improved the working conditions of his employees.

Humphrey Noyes, became the director of Oneida. Pierrepont, who had started a successful business in wholesale silverware in New York City, turned the corporation around by selling off its unprofitable divisions and focusing on its most successful product—tableware. That move helped to save the company.

The idea of Oneida as a community of like-minded people also survived, although Noyes's utopian ideals and Perfectionist beliefs were gradually forgotten. The company paid employees good wages, organized various social activities, and encouraged them to work for a common good. During hard times, managers as well as their subordinates worked longer hours and took cuts in their pay.

During the good times, all employees were rewarded with generous raises, shorter work weeks, and additional benefits such as stock in the company.

In a new community known as Sherrill, near Oneida, the company offered bonuses to help its employees build their own homes. Another district, Kenwood, was built to house the former Oneidans and their descendants, while the utopian community of Oneida was transformed into a loosely organized residential neighborhood. Gradually, the original community disappeared, as outsiders bought homes in Sherrill and Kenwood. By the 1960s, most employees of Oneida, Ltd. (as it is now known) had no ties to the Perfectionist society of John Humphrey Noyes, and the company itself had joined the mainstream of American businesses.

Oneida is still respected today for its tableware.

Regal in bearing, Katherine Tingley (1847-1929)
captivated artists and industrialists alike and built
an elegant modern utopia in southern California.

7

Katherine Tingley
The Point Loma Community

*A*s the modern industrial era brought rapid and drastic change to people throughout the United States and Europe, thousands sought to find stability in their lives by renewing their religious commitments—or by exploring new forms of spirituality. A Russian woman named Helena Petrovna Blavatsky traveled the world in her spiritual quests. In the United States, Colonel Henry Steel Olcott, a lawyer by training, wrote newspaper articles on *séances*, meetings in which people attempted to communicate with the dead. The two were drawn together by

*With her mysterious past and claims of contacting the
"Masters," Helena Petrovna Blavatsky (1831-1891)
was an odd partner for Colonel Henry Steel Olcott
(1832-1907), a Civil War veteran and family man.
But the two spiritual seekers were so inseparable that
people called them the Theosophical Twins.*

their fascination for unexplained psychic phenomena and
spiritualism, the belief in communication with the dead.

Since the late 1840s, séances had been popular with
people attempting to speak with their dead loved ones.
Although interest in supernatural phenomena was waning
by the 1870s, Blavatsky and Olcott dedicated their lives to
the study of the *occult*, or supernatural knowledge.
Together with 14 other searchers, Olcott and Blavatsky
formed the Theosophical Society in Blavatsky's New York

City apartment one night in 1875. Little did they know that Theosophy—which meant "divine wisdom"—would become a worldwide religious movement.

Soon both Blavatsky and Olcott rejected spiritualism as fraudulent and devoted themselves solely to studying Theosophy. They believed that the same divine wisdom was the basis of all of the world's religions, including Buddhism, Hinduism, Islam, and Christianity. Wise men living in India's Himalaya Mountains—whom they called "Masters" or "Adepts" or "Mahatmas"—had preserved the original knowledge underlying these religious traditions. Blavatsky had met with the Masters in Tibet, she claimed, and she continued to have an occult connection with them. She planned to make their wisdom available to the world again. Theosophy's study of this universal spiritual knowledge, Blavatsky and her followers contended, might help unite the world's nations in peace.

In 1877, Blavatsky published *Isis Unveiled*, a two-volume compilation of the Masters' teachings. After she and Olcott left for India the following year, the remaining Theosophists in the United States continued their studies under the leadership of William Quan Judge, a lawyer who was one of the group's founding members. Blavatsky was still their spiritual inspiration, and her 1888 work, *The Secret Doctrine*, is considered to be the central text of the Theosophical Society to this day. *The Secret Doctrine* revealed the source of the world's religious traditions and also detailed the Theosophists' belief in reincarnation and the possibility of evolving into Masters who could save the world with their knowledge.

Thousands of people around the world pored over Blavatsky's works and became Theosophists. One of these avid readers was Katherine Tingley. Born in 1847 and raised in Newburyport, Massachusetts, Tingley had felt a fascination for the occult early in her life. She had an equally strong interest in social reform. When she was living in New York City in the late 1880s, Tingley founded a charitable association, the Ladies' Society of Mercy, whose members paid visits to hospital patients and prison inmates. The society was supported by readings and dramatic presentations organized by Tingley, who was a trained actress. Tingley also served at séances as a *medium*, a person who contacts the spirits of the dead.

Late in 1892 or early in 1893, Tingley met William Judge while working at the Do-Good Mission, an organization she had founded to provide food for the city's poor. When Judge introduced her to Blavatsky's work, Tingley was immediately taken with Theosophy, which combined a way of improving human life with spiritual exploration. Her charitable work, Tingley felt, was not "removing the causes of misery." Theosophy showed how spiritual enlightenment could save humanity.

These years were difficult for Judge, and he leaned heavily on his new friend. After Helena Blavatsky's death in 1891, Judge had fallen into a struggle for power over the Theosophical Society with Olcott, who was still in

An Irish immigrant and Gaelic mystic, William Quan Judge (1851-1896) had been one of Helena Blavatsky's closest associates. He believed that Blavatsky communicated with him through Tingley.

India, and Annie Besant, a recent convert who headed the group in England. There were more Theosophists in the United States than anywhere else, but Olcott and Besant wanted to take the vice-presidency of the organization away from Judge. Finally, in 1895, Judge made the Theosophical Society in America an independent group.

Judge's health had suffered from the stress of the conflict, however, and he died in March 1896 without naming a successor to lead the American Theosophists. Always clad in a purple gown, with her dark hair piled high on her head, Katherine Tingley had made a powerful impression on the Theosophists during her short time with the group. At the séances she held with the other Theosophical leaders, she made contact with Judge's spirit and announced his wish to see her become Outer Head of the Esoteric Section, the position Helena Blavatsky had held until her death. Convinced by Tingley's revelation, the other members chose her to lead the group, although they kept the choice secret for several months. Annie Besant, who had relocated to India, also claimed this title, and her Adyar branch of Theosophy would feud with the Americans for many years to come.

At the 1896 Theosophical Society convention, Tingley, who had not yet been announced as Outer Head, proposed an international center of Theosophy, which would be called the School for the Revival of the Lost Mysteries of Antiquity. Tingley's plan was revolutionary. Instead of merely a place for the study of Theosophy, this school would be a utopian community founded to help members develop into Masters. The center of the community would be a boarding school for children, whose graduates would eventually be ready to establish their own Theosophical centers around the world.

Tingley explained her vision to the excited crowd. "When Theosophy has liberated all men," she predicted, "the prisons will be emptied, wars will cease, hunger and famine will be unknown." Instead of strife, declared Tingley, "all mankind will abide in peace, unity, and love." Enthralled, Theosophists pledged $5,000 toward the plan.

Where was the best place for such a community? Blavatsky had predicted that a society of Masters would develop in the United States. Now Tingley found the perfect spot. Point Loma, a peninsula in California on the western side of the San Diego harbor, would be the future site of her utopian Theosophical community.

With several other leaders of the society, Tingley set out in 1896 on a round-the-world tour to announce the founding of Point Loma. Throughout Europe, she made speeches and held suppers for the poor, hoping to draw Europeans to the American Theosophists instead of the competing faction in India. At every location, she selected stones to be used in the building of Point Loma to symbolize the international foundation of the community.

Tingley then made a sojourn to Egypt and to India, the fabled homes of the Masters. While Annie Besant claimed that the Adyars living in India were the true Theosophists, Tingley countered that Theosophy had been founded in the United States. But she had more important things to do in India than argue with Besant. After hiking alone into the foothills of the Himalayas, Tingley reported that she had met with one of the Masters. Such a meeting was crucial for her as Outer Head of the Esoteric Section because she needed to be able to establish contact with the "Inner Heads"—the Masters—in her search for ancient wisdom.

The successful trip to India completed, Tingley led the group to Australia and New Zealand. Then, in January 1897, they crossed the Pacific Ocean to the California coast, where 132 acres of land had been purchased on Point Loma. The new community, which they called "Lomaland," would expand to nearly 500 acres in the coming years. In February, Tingley presided over the laying of Point Loma's first cornerstone, in which she placed documents about the founding and early history of the Theosophical Society. Hundreds of townspeople and the mayor of San Diego came to witness the ceremony.

While construction proceeded on the school and other buildings, Tingley led another fundraising tour, this time across the United States. A charismatic and intense woman, Tingley impressed many wealthy patrons, and large numbers of artists, intellectuals, lawyers, and businessmen were attracted to Theosophy.

Tingley organized the International Brotherhood League to continue her charitable work in April 1897. The group founded the Lotus Home for poor children living in New York City. The next year, the Brotherhood set up a relief camp on Long Island for wounded and ill veterans of the Spanish-American War. Tingley also traveled to war-torn Cuba to help with the relief effort there.

In 1897 and 1898, Tingley had to deal with the first major division in the Theosophical Society in America. Ernest Hargrove, who had become president after the death of William Judge, resigned in August 1897 to start a competing organization. Although he had joined with the other leaders in making Tingley the Outer Head, Hargrove was suspicious of Tingley's claim that she had spoken with a Master. Hargrove tried to gain converts, but his group remained small.

Tingley's efficiently organized camps for soldiers wounded in the Spanish-American War prompted a New York newspaper to call her "a Soldier's Angel."

By the time of the 1898 convention, Tingley's leadership of the newly renamed Universal Brotherhood and Theosophical Society was virtually assured. Meeting as a committee, Tingley's strongest backers approved the new constitution she had drafted. The membership had not been allowed to debate the constitution, but they voted it in by an overwhelming majority of 290 to 24. Tingley was now president for life. She alone had the power to hire and fire the society's officials, decide on all the society's laws, and make any amendments to the constitution.

Since the founding of the Theosophical Society in 1875, groups around the world had formed local lodges that were run independently. After the 1898 convention, however, Tingley shut down many lodges across the United States because they were pursuing psychic phenomena, which she now rejected. Others closed because they turned to Adyar or came to distrust Tingley. The Universal Brotherhood and Theosophical Society soon became headquartered at Point Loma.

In April 1899, Tingley moved from New York City to Point Loma. The new Theosophical community was inaugurated with great fanfare, and lectures, concerts, and plays were presented during a 10-day Theosophical Society congress. The huge hotel they had built was soon remodeled to become the glass-domed Homestead (later the Raja Yoga Academy), and a lovely round Temple topped with a dome made of amethyst-colored glass was erected. Cottages supplemented the Homestead's living quarters. Using international architectural styles to reflect the idea of universal wisdom, Tingley helped design an Egyptian gate leading to the nation's first Greek theater. Hindu and Muslim features decorated Point Loma's halls and homes, and the stones that Tingley had collected from around the world were erected as two tall pillars. Lomaland looked like a brand-new world.

Tingley carefully screened new members, who paid a hefty $500 fee to move to Point Loma. In the early years, Point Loma was home to several hundred permanent residents and drew well-known novelists, painters, poets, and educators. Many of them were interested in Theosophy, while others simply wanted to try communal

The Greek theater at Point Loma was built in 1901 for innovative theater performances that included dancing, processions, and choruses in the style of the ancient Greek dramas.

living. Members wore uniforms and diligently performed their work, avoiding unnecessary conversation as they focused on improving themselves. Theosophy taught that with enough study and effort people could develop the occult powers known to the Masters.

Even though Lomalanders were intent on evolving into higher states of spiritual consciousness, much of this process was fun. The Isis League presented *symposia* in which actors playing historical philosophers and artists had imaginary conversations, as well as concerts, parades, Greek drama, and Shakespeare's plays. The music and dance programs at Point Loma were renowned for their uniqueness and superb quality, and writers and artists found a haven there for their work. Many artists repaid the community with designs for furniture and building interiors. Lectures and conferences were also held frequently at Point Loma and in San Diego.

The Theosophists were just as innovative when it came to agriculture. Determined to turn the dry, nearly rainless land into an oasis of fertility, they built a large irrigation system and planted pine forests, fruit orchards, vegetable gardens, and fields of wheat and oats. A grove of eucalyptus trees was planted along the bluffs to serve as a windbreak. In addition to farming, Lomaland had cultivated over 1,000 varieties of garden plants and planted thousands of trees to make new forests by the 1920s. The experimental work of Theosophical agriculturalists made a tremendous contribution to the agricultural economy of California.

The community's workshops produced clothing, fine textiles, and leather goods. A Women's Exchange and Mart sewed all the community's uniforms. Blacksmith and woodworking shops were housed with the Mart in the Industrial Building, as was a printing company. The works of Helena Blavatsky and Katherine Tingley and other Theosophical books, magazines, and pamphlets, were published there, and the Theosophical Publishing Company became respected for its fine printing.

To Tingley, the Theosophical boarding school was critical because the younger a person began studying the ancient wisdom, the greater the chance to develop into a

Master. She named the school the Raja Yoga Academy, from the Sanskrit words for "royal union." Raja Yoga students studied academic subjects, learned trades, practiced music, and participated in athletics. Students as young as two years of age attended math and spelling classes. Groups of 6 to 12 children lived apart from their parents in small cottages overseen by teachers, who directed all their academic and recreational activities.

Poor children and orphans from the United States and Cuba made up the tiny first class in 1900, and more than 2,500 students were educated at Point Loma during its existence. Tingley intended to spread her Raja Yoga system around the world. In the first decade of the twentieth century, she opened new schools in San Francisco and San Diego, as well as in the Cuban cities of Santiago, Pinar del Río, and Santa Clara. Tingley made plans to build a school on San Juan Hill, the site of a famous battle during the Spanish-American War. She also bought property for schools in England and Sweden. In the 1920s, Tingley purchased land for institutions in Massachusetts, Minnesota, and Germany. When the Raja Yoga students at Point Loma began graduating, she opened the Theosophical University in 1919.

But Tingley also suffered setbacks. In 1906, the San Francisco earthquake destroyed a Raja Yoga school, and the San Diego academy lasted only a few years. By 1912, with revolution sweeping Cuba, the last of the Cuban Raja Yoga schools closed.

Unlike most utopian experiments, Point Loma was deeply involved with social problems outside its boundaries. Tingley campaigned against capital punishment and *vivisection*, the practice of experimenting on live animals. Lomalanders convinced the state of Arizona to ban hanging temporarily, calling instead for prison reform to help criminals become better human beings.

Tingley also strongly opposed war. In 1913, she organized an international Theosophical peace congress in Sweden. The next year, following the outbreak of World War I in Europe, she asked President Woodrow Wilson to sanction a Sacred Peace Day. To publicize the proposed holiday, she led a huge parade of soldiers, students, and civic leaders through the streets of San Diego. Although President Wilson denied her request, Tingley continued to hold peace conferences and fought the drafting of Raja Yoga students into the armed forces after the United States entered the war in 1917.

By that time, some of the wealthy donors, as well as some Theosophical leaders, were becoming disturbed by Tingley's near-dictatorial powers. Tingley had appointed a cabinet of advisors and managers, but she still made all important decisions herself. Some members complained that she spent far more than the society could afford on lavish theater productions and new schools. Others, influenced by Adyar and other Theosophical leaders who had split from Tingley, questioned her interpretation of Helena Blavatsky's original teachings.

Because Point Loma never came close to meeting its own economic needs, Tingley constantly had to struggle with debt and convince people to donate money.

Many of Tingley's followers left the Universal Brotherhood and joined the rival Theosophical group at Adyar in India in the 1920s. As membership in the Universal Brotherhood declined, Point Loma began to lose income. Tingley also became snarled in lawsuits. Irene Mohn, the wife of a Theosophist patron named George Mohn, sued Tingley for $200,000, accusing the Point Loma leader of breaking up her marriage. Tingley's legal bills mounted as the case dragged on in California's courts for several years. Finally, the California Supreme Court decided against Tingley, and she was forced to take out loans in order to pay the judgment.

In May 1929, Katherine Tingley was in a car accident while traveling in Germany. The injuries worsened her already poor health, and she died on July 11. That autumn, the stock-market crash put an end to the remaining support Point Loma had received from its wealthy donors. The once beautiful gardens and orchards became overgrown, and the community fell into disrepair. During the next few years, residents of Point Loma left the community as the society sold off the buildings and the land.

In the meantime, the Universal Brotherhood cabinet selected Gottfried de Purucker as Tingley's successor. A scholar of Sanskrit, the ancient Indian language in which the sacred texts of Hinduism were written, Purucker took more interest in study than in the community's musical or dramatic presentations. He also began a halting process of reconciliation with Adyar, which in the long run probably helped both organizations survive.

Purucker could not save Point Loma, however. By 1932, the worst year of the Depression, the Point Loma community was not even able to pay its taxes. Under Purucker's leadership, it continued to struggle for several years until the entire property was sold to meet its debts. Purucker moved the society to Covina, east of Los Angeles, in 1942. The estate at Point Loma was still a fine campus, and Balboa University was established there after World War II. Point Loma's buildings later housed California Western University, and Point Loma Nazarene University moved to the site in 1973.

Katherine Tingley's former residence is now Cabrillo Hall, home to the Communication Studies Department at Point Loma Nazarene University.

With a new wave of spiritual books appearing since the 1970s, Theosophy has enjoyed a revival. New Age writers examine past lives, unexplained supernatural phenomena, psychic powers, and the possibility of contacting the dead or prophets of the past. Helena Blavatsky's books on the ancient wisdom of the Masters again have found a wide audience. While Lomaland has disappeared, Theosophists still follow the teachings of Katherine Tingley and other early leaders. Theosophists in the two major Theosophical groups—both of which call themselves the Theosophical Society—are active in hundreds of branches and lodges all over the world.

Karl Marx (1818-1883) introduced a new realm of utopian thought when he predicted that laboring people worldwide would gain power over wealthy owners of land and industry.

8

Modern Utopian Communities

Many utopian communities were in decline by the end of the 1800s. Their original members quit or died off, and most children brought up in these utopias left their communities upon reaching adulthood. The strict discipline, peculiar doctrines, and austere lifestyle of many religious utopians discouraged outsiders from joining.

The nation's rapid growth and industrialization also hurt American utopias. As the population and wealth of the United States increased, the value of agricultural land rose, making it more costly for utopians to expand or to start new communities. American industry emphasized mass production of inexpensive consumer goods, so the markets for fine handmade products such as Shaker brooms and Amana woolens decreased. A few utopias, such as Oneida and Amana, followed the lead of big business by focusing on manufacturing and transformed themselves into corporations in order to compete.

The growing class of industrial workers was as concerned about social inequalities and achieving a decent standard of living as the utopians had been, but many placed their hopes in a complete change of government— a socialist or communist society. Some laborers dreamed

William D. "Big Bill" Haywood (1869-1928) was one of the founders of Industrial Workers of the World, a worldwide labor union that sought to make the whole world a utopia ruled by workers.

In Looking Backward, *Edward Bellamy (1850-1898) imagined the world in the year 2000 under a socialist utopian government. His vision was so captivating that clubs started across the nation to achieve his goal.*

of putting the political power of an entire nation—and eventually the world—in the hands of workers. *Looking Backward*, an 1888 novel by Edward Bellamy, proposed just such a socialist utopia and inspired a few short-lived real communities. So did *The Communist Manifesto* (1848) and *Das Kapital* (published in several volumes beginning in 1867), two works by social philosopher Karl Marx, whose "scientific utopia" was the model for the revolutionaries who overthrew the Russian tsar in 1917.

The Soviet Union they created was, of course, no utopia. Observing the dangers of societies like the Soviet Union and Fascist nations in Europe, writers of the twentieth century created nightmarish imaginary utopias called *dystopias.* Aldous Huxley wrote *Brave New World* in 1932, and George Orwell's book *1984* appeared 17 years later. Unlike the idealized societies of Sir Thomas More's 1516 *Utopia* and Bellamy's *Looking Backward*, the imaginary worlds in these two works were oppressive societies. Their dictators were modeled on real-life Fascists and Communists such as the Soviet Union's Josef Stalin, Italy's Benito Mussolini, and Germany's Adolf Hitler. Freedom and creativity were banned in these fictional societies, and the state carefully monitored its citizens and punished those who thought or acted independently.

But not all utopias of the twentieth century were nightmares. In the early 1900s, small, self-sustaining communities known as *kibbutzim* were established in what is now the nation of Israel. Several hundred kibbutzim still exist today and produce a large percentage of Israel's food. Their members grow crops and work in small industries that help the community earn money from the outside world. The families who belong to a kibbutz live and work together and send their children to the kibbutz's own school. People from all over the world who were interested in living in self-sufficient communities visited the kibbutzim of Israel during the 1960s. The kibbutzim are different from many nineteenth century utopias in that their members are as committed to the nation of Israel as they are to the kibbutzim.

Some of the people most intrigued by the kibbutzim were American students in the 1960s. These young men

In the early twentieth century, the Zionist movement for a Jewish nation developed the kibbutz, the most successful form of commune in the world. Kibbutz members raise the Israeli flag each day, showing their dedication to the nation of Israel.

and women, who had grown up in the prosperous era after World War II, yearned for a simpler and more spiritual life. At universities across the United States, there developed a counterculture of students opposing authority figures, a capitalistic economy, and the involvement of the United States in the Vietnam War.

The members of this counterculture wanted a society that gave up middle-class comforts in favor of manual labor and self-sufficiency. Many of them found inspiration in the writings of utopian George Ripley's friend Henry David Thoreau, whose 1854 book, *Walden*, had described his search for a simpler existence. For two years, Thoreau left behind the bustle and stress of the city for a quieter, independent life in the countryside.

The first utopian communities of the counterculture were urban homes in which members agreed to share everything. In the late 1960s, dozens of small communes were set up in San Francisco's Haight-Ashbury neighborhood. Others began in Los Angeles, New York City, and in many college towns. Eventually, many urban utopians moved out of the cities to start communes in rural areas. More than 1,000 communes had been established in the United States by the end of the decade.

Most of these communes failed quickly, but the few that survived had one thing in common—a strong leader. In the early 1960s, a utopian visionary and college professor named Stephen Gaskin gave weekly lectures and held open discussions about the state of society and what a more livable community would be like. Audiences of hundreds of people in San Francisco, a center of the counterculture movement, came to hear him. In October 1970, Gaskin organized a cross-country tour, nicknamed "the Caravan," and set off with several hundred young people to promote his ideas. Eleven months later, the group decided to move to Summertown, Tennessee, to settle a rural commune they named the Farm.

Members of the Farm held a wide variety of religious beliefs. While some of them followed Buddhism, others were Christians. But instead of seizing on any particular doctrine, members experimented with the

Carrying on the tradition of his weekly lectures in San Francisco, Stephen Gaskin continued to be the religious leader of the Farm. Central to his beliefs, however, is the idea that anyone can be a spiritual teacher.

world's religions like explorers searching for an ideal faith. Individuals followed their own conscience in religion as well as in other aspects of their lives. These modern utopians would have firmly rejected the strict teachings of the Shakers or the Inspirationists.

Like many members of the counterculture, Gaskin and his followers often used marijuana and psychedelic drugs. Marijuana grown on the property was, in fact, a regular part of their religious ceremonies. In the early 1970s, narcotics police raided the commune. Gaskin and

Members come to the Farm's clinic, run by the commune's own physicians, to immunize their children. Women in the surrounding Tennessee area also go there to give birth.

several other members were charged with drug possession and spent time in jail. But the arrests and outside interference did not discourage Gaskin and the members of the Farm. Gaskin's community is still in operation today, with several hundred members working either at the Farm's handful of small industries or in nearby towns.

Although most of the modern utopians had little faith in religious, political, or social doctrines, a few did form communities based on the teachings of anarchism, which holds that the best society rejects all rulers and doctrines. The philosophy of anarchism dated back several hundred years and had inspired several short-lived utopias in the 1920s. In the summer of 1967, a dozen New York anarchists moved north to a remote valley of Vermont to settle Cold Mountain Farm. The members believed that without a set plan or rules and without a designated leader, each of them would be free to best utilize his or her talents. The only rule at Cold Mountain Farm was that no member could be forced to leave.

The members of Cold Mountain Farm wanted to become completely self-sufficient by growing their own food and making their own goods. But none of them had any experience as farmers. They were uncertain when to plant or harvest crops and were not used to the difficult work of plowing and weeding large plots of land. When their equipment broke down, they were unable to repair it. They also earned the suspicion and hostility of their neighbors by working outside in the nude.

Gradually, the group grew more isolated from the world and their supporters in New York, but then several new residents arrived from the city. With the farmhouse too small to hold them, new private residences were built on the property, which lessened the feeling of community. Any member who was troublesome remained a burden at Cold Mountain Farm because no one could be forced to leave. An outbreak of hepatitis occurred that summer, and by autumn many of the residents drifted back to New York or to other communes in New England.

In the summer of 1968, about 30 members of the Cold Mountain commune moved to a new property in Vermont called Bryn Athyn. The members of this group were more cohesive. Benefiting from a little more experience, they carried out the needed farming tasks and for a time managed to support themselves. But Bryn Athyn also attracted the attention of federal agents, who arrived in search of men evading the military draft.

At the end of the summer, most members of Bryn Athyn moved across the country to New Mexico. Several dozen small communes had already been built in the remote mountain valleys of that state, where members of the counterculture felt safe from the mainstream society they despised and from law-enforcement officials. A few Bryn Athyn members joined one such commune, which was named Placitas.

Under the guidance of an engineer named Steve Baer, Placitas members had built two geodesic domes as living quarters. (The domes, which were invented by the American scientist and utopian thinker R. Buckminster Fuller, were supposed to provide an ideal living environment.) But Placitas eventually split into two separate communities that had little contact with each other, and members gradually drifted away from both. In December 1970, two people at Placitas were murdered by outsiders. After this incident, the commune broke up for good. Baer moved to Albuquerque, New Mexico, and started a business that manufactured geodesic domes.

Small religious utopias have also survived in the United States. Many are based on eastern religions such as Buddhism or Hinduism. Others are Christian retreats, modeled on the self-contained monastic communities that have dotted the Middle East and Europe since the beginning of Christianity. Some are *cults*, in which a single leader dominates his followers, demanding strict obedience and total withdrawal from the rest of society. Cults can be dangerous, and several in the last few decades have ended in mass suicides.

Today, some utopians plan societies in a place unlike any that George Rapp, Robert Owen, or Katherine Tingley could possibly have imagined—the computer screen. Computer games like Sim City, My City, and Civilization put users in the position of creating or reconstructing cities or even whole cultures. Introduced by a company called Maxis in 1989, Sim City was the first computer game for city planning. The original game

A utopian city created with Sim City 3000

and Sim City 2000 have sold millions of copies worldwide and are translated into over a dozen languages. Each year since 1993, the National Engineer's Week Future Cities Competition challenges students in schools across the nation to create a city using Sim City 2000 to solve a pressing urban problem such as transportation, pollution, or education. Students then build models of their cities and present them in the competition, with the finalists displaying their creations in Washington, D.C.

Some of these computer games, including Ultima Online, Civilization, and Asheron's Call, have versions of their games that allow players to interact (or compete) with other players on the Internet. The Internet has potentially unlimited possibilities for future utopians. It can allow like-minded people with modems to gather together electronically to share their backgrounds, beliefs, ideas, and plans. They can even create virtual communities in which people have relationships and take action on issues that concern them.

Some Internet networks or sites have such unlikely names as Usenet, MUDs, and the WELL. Others are more descriptively called "bulletin boards" or "chat rooms." WELL stands for Whole Earth 'Lectronic Link and is an offshoot of the Whole Earth Catalog, which originated from the 1960s commune counterculture in San Francisco. The WELL now, like the Whole Earth Catalog then, meets networking needs by hosting "conferences" ranging from fan clubs to parents' groups and posting information on electronic bulletin boards. The WELL and Usenet both carry thousands of "newsgroups," through which people around the world can post or receive information with no censorship and at minimal cost. Anyone with bulletin-board system software can also create a bulletin board, and many people use them for grassroots community organizing. Other groups, especially environmental activists, use computer-mediated communications software to organize protests internationally with little expense. The applications for this technology are endless.

If the WELL, Usenet, bulletin boards, and other computer technology make it possible for people to work together on real-world problems and interests, MUDs (Multi-User Dungeons), MOOs (object-oriented MUDs), and MUSEs (Multi-User Simulated Environments) allow users to create virtual communities of a sort on the Internet. They are usually games or adventures, in which characters created by users interact. On many of these sites, wizards and warlocks battle dragons and evil spirits, but MUDs can also be more serious. People logging on to LambdaMOO, for example, take part in a place that functions something like a society, complete with a form of government. Closer yet to a utopian virtual community is MicroMUSE's Cyberion City, which requests its citizens to create buildings or other objects (such as rain forests) that will serve the needs of the city.

To create an ideal imaginary world was the goal of writers from Sir Thomas More to Edward Bellamy. Now, through computer technology and the Internet, users from around the world can explore new electronic communities or work to save their own real-life communities in the comfort of their own homes. With advanced technology, online utopians of today and in the future can take advantage of adding audio and visual elements to their Internet societies. Other visionaries have new tools to make the existing world a better place. What may result is a utopia more diverse and promising than any other this world has ever seen.

Utopians in Their Own Words

In this book, you have read about a wide range of religious and social utopians. The following are excerpts from the writings of some of the leaders of utopian societies described in the previous chapters. The excerpts include reasons for establishing a particular community, rules of personal conduct within a society, and the dream of achieving a perfect fellowship of believers. Although the methods of each group varied greatly, each shared a common goal of achieving more meaningful human relationships through practicing a simpler, more disciplined lifestyle.

Introduction:

The Ancient Greeks
"Unless the philosophers rule as kings or those now called kings and chiefs genuinely and adequately philosophize, and political power and philosophy coincide in the same place . . . [then] there is no rest from ills for the cities . . . nor I think for human kind."

—Socrates, from Plato's *Republic*, 4th century B.C.

Sir Thomas More
"The island of Utopia is in the middle 200 miles broad . . . but it grows narrower at both ends. There are fifty-four cities in the island, all large and well built: the manners, customs, and laws of which are the same. But lest any city should become too great . . . provision is made that none of their cities may contain above 6,000 families. No family may have less than ten and more than sixteen persons in it; but there can be no determined number for the children under age."

—Thomas More, *Utopia*, 1516

Chapter 1: The Shakers

"O my dear children, hold fast, and be not discouraged. God has not sent us into this land in vain; but He has sent us to bring the gospel to this nation, who are deeply lost in sin; and there are great numbers who will embrace it, and the time draws nigh."

—Ann Lee, c. 1779

"All the members of the Church have a just and equal right to the use of things, according to their order and needs; no other difference ought to be made, between Elder or younger in things spiritual or temporal, than that which is just, and is for the peace and unity, and good of the whole."

—Joseph Meacham, c. 1792

Chapter 2: Harmony

"The simple object sought is to approximate, so far as human imperfections may allow, . . . the fulfillment of the will of God, by the exercise of those affections and the practice of those virtues which are essential to the happiness of man in time and throughout eternity."

—From the Articles of Association, 1805

"On my journey, I became so weary of the world and particularly of the city life, that I am glad to live again among my friends, who have uprightness for their rule, and, where instead of fashionable luxury, simple frugality governs the rudder."

—Frederick Rapp, upon returning to Harmony, 1817

Chapter 3: New Harmony

"In the Manufacturing Towns,—the poor and working classes now usually live in garrets or cellars, within narrow lanes or confined courts.

In the Proposed Villages,—the poor and working classes will live in dwellings formed into a large square, rendered in every way convenient, and usefully ornamented.

In the Manufacturing Towns,—the children [are] trained under ignorant persons, possessing many bad habits.

In the Proposed Villages,—the children will be trained by intelligent persons, possessing only good habits."

—Robert Owen, in a letter to London newspapers, 1817

"The New Moral World is an organization to rationally educate and employ all, through a new organization of society which will give a new existence to man by surrounding him with superior circumstances only."

—Robert Owen, *The Book of the New Moral World*, 1836

Chapter 4: The Amana Colonies

"Every member of this Society is in duty bound to hand over his or her personal and real property to the Trustees for the common fund, at the time of his or her acceptance as a member, and before the signing of this Constitution."

—Article V, Amana Society Constitution, 1859

"Have no pleasure in violent games or plays; do not wait on the road to look at quarrels or fights; do not keep company with bad children, for there you will learn only wickedness. Also, do not play with children of the other sex."

—From the catechism for Inspirationist children, c. 1850s

Chapter 5: Brook Farm

"[We wish] to insure a more natural union between intellectual and manual labor than now exists; to combine the thinker and the worker, as far as possible, in the same individual; to guarantee the highest mental freedoms, by providing all with labor adapted to their tastes and talents . . . and to prepare a society of liberal, intelligent, and cultivated persons, whose relations with each other would permit a more wholesome and simple life than can be led amidst the pressures of our competitive institutions. . . . To accomplish these objects, we propose to take a small tract of land which . . . will be adequate to the subsistence of the families; and to connect with this a school or college, in which the most complete instruction shall be given, from the first rudiments to the highest culture."

—George Ripley, in a letter to Ralph Waldo Emerson, November 1840

"A true life, although it aims beyond the highest star, is redolent of the healthy earth. The perfume of clover lingers about it. The lowing of cattle is the natural bass to the melody of human voices. On the other hand, what absurdity can be imagined greater than the institution of cities? They originated not in love, but in war. It was war that drove men together in multitudes, and compelled them to stand so close, and build walls around them. This crowded condition produces wants of unnatural character, which resulted in occupations that regenerated the evil, by creating artificial wants."

—From an essay in the *Dial* magazine, 1842

Chapter 6: Oneida

"We do not belong to ourselves in any respect, but . . . we do belong to God, and second to Mr. Noyes as God's true representative. . . . We will, if necessary . . . cheerfully resign all desire to become mothers, if for any reason Mr. Noyes deems us unfit material for propagation."

—From the resolutions to which women were asked to agree upon joining the Oneida community, c. 1860s

"The truth is, the way of salvation is more valuable than pain in its results; and the way that Christ proposes to save us, on the whole, is not by suffering, but by making us happy. The happiest man is the best man, and does the most good."

—John Humphrey Noyes, 1875

Chapter 7: Point Loma

"In the golden land, far away, by the blue Pacific, I thought as a child that I could fashion a city and bring the people of all countries together and have the youth taught how to live, and how to become true and strong and noble, and forceful royal warriors for humanity."

—Katherine Tingley

"When Theosophy has liberated all men . . . the prisons will be emptied, wars will cease, hunger and famine will be unknown; . . . disease, which so often springs from evil acts and thoughts, will pass away . . . and under the shadowing wings of the great brotherhood, all mankind will abide in peace, unity, and love."

—Katherine Tingley, 1896

Bibliography

Andrews, Edward Deming. *The People Called Shakers: A Search for the Perfect Society.* New York: Oxford University Press, 1953.

Barthel, Diane L. *Amana: From Pietist Sect to American Community.* Lincoln: University of Nebraska Press, 1984.

Carden, Maren Lockwood. *Oneida: Utopian Community to Modern Corporation.* Baltimore: Johns Hopkins University Press, 1969.

Curtis, Edith Roelker. *A Season in Utopia: The Story of Brook Farm.* New York: Russel & Russel, 1961.

Duss, John S. *The Harmonists: A Personal History.* Harrisburg: Pennsylvania Book Service, 1943.

Fogarty, Robert S. *American Utopianism.* Itasca, Ill.: Peacock, 1972.

Gardner, Hugh. *The Children of Prosperity: Thirteen Modern American Communes.* New York: St. Martin's, 1978.

Greenwalt, Emmett A. *The Point Loma Community in California, 1897-1942: A Theosophical Experiment.* Berkeley: University of California Press, 1955.

Holloway, Mark. *Heavens on Earth: Utopian Communities in America, 1680-1880.* London: Turnstile, 1951.

Knoedler, Christiana F. *The Harmony Society.* New York: Vantage, 1954.

Lawson, Donna. *Brothers and Sisters All over This Land.* New York: Praeger, 1972.

Lockwood, George B. *The New Harmony Movement.* New York: Appleton, 1905.

Melville, Keith. *Communes in the Counter Culture: Origins, Theories, Styles of Life.* New York: William Morrow, 1972.

More, Thomas. *Utopia.* 1516. Reprint, translated and with an introduction by Paul Turner, New York: Penguin, 1965.

Nordhoff, Charles. *The Communistic Societies of the United States.* 1875. Reprint, New York: Schocken, 1965.

Oved, Yaacov. *Two Hundred Years of American Communes.* New Brunswick, N.J.: Transaction, 1988.

Plato. *The Republic.* Translated and with an essay by Allan David Bloom. New York: Basic, 1968.

Pollard, Sidney, and John Salt, eds. *Robert Owen: Prophet of the Poor.* Lewisburg, Penn.: Bucknell University Press, 1971.

Rheingold, Howard. *The Virtual Community: Home-steading on the Electronic Frontier.* Reading, Mass.: Addison-Wesley, 1993.

Ryan, Charles J. *H. P. Blavatsky and the Theosophical Movement: A Brief Historical Sketch.* Pasadena, Calif.: Theosophical University Press, 1975.

Shambaugh, Bertha M. H. *Amana: The Community of True Inspiration.* Des Moines: State Historical Society of Iowa, 1988.

Swift, Lindsay. *Brook Farm: Its Members, Scholars, and Visitors.* New York: Corinth, 1961.

Veysey, Laurence R. *The Communal Experience: Anarchist and Mystical Counter-Culture in America.* New York: Harper & Row, 1973.

Wilson, William E. *The Angel and the Serpent.* Bloomington: Indiana University Press, 1964.

Index

157

ABOUT THE AUTHOR

TOM STREISSGUTH, who was born in Washington, D.C., in 1958, graduated from Yale University, where he studied history, literature, languages, and music. He has traveled widely in Europe and the Middle East and has been a teacher, editor, and journalist. Streissguth is also the author of The Oliver Press books *Charismatic Cult Leaders*, *Communications: Sending the Message*, *Hatemongers and Demagogues*, *Hoaxers and Hustlers*, *International Terrorists*, *Legendary Labor Leaders*, and *Soviet Leaders from Lenin to Gorbachev*. He lives in Sarasota, Florida, with his wife and two daughters.

The publisher wishes to thank the following individuals and organizations for their careful review of parts of this book:
Patricia A. Leiphart and Raymond Shepherd, Old Economy Village of the Pennsylvania Historical and Museum Commission; Amana Heritage Society; and Gina Stankivitz, Collections Manager/Educator, Oneida Community Mansion House.

Photo Credits
Photographs courtesy of: pp. 6, 9, 11, 18, 34, 35, 39, 42, 45, 49, 50, 56, 59, 61, 63, 80, 82, 89, 90 (both), 95, 96, 99, 105, 132, 134, Library of Congress; pp. 14, 20, 23, 25, 27, 28, 31, Shaker Museum and Library, Old Chatham, New York; pp. 32, 43, 46, 47, Old Economy Village, Pennsylvania Historical and Museum Commission; p. 41, Revilo; p. 53, State Archives, Indiana Commission on Public Records; pp. 64, 70, 71, 72, 73, 74, 76, 78, 79, Amana Heritage Society, Amana, Iowa; p. 66, Bundesarchiv; p. 88, Concord Free Public Library, Concord, Mass.; p. 94, Boston Public Library; pp. 103, 104, 107, 110, 112, Oneida Community Mansion House; p. 113, Oneida, Ltd., Oneida, N.Y.; pp. 114, 137, 139, 140, UPI/Corbis-Bettmann; pp. 116 (both), 119, 129, 135, *Dictionary of American Portraits*; p. 123, National Archives; pp. 125, 131, Communications Office, Point Loma Nazarene University; p. 144, Maxis.